ℓp

Inventing a Nation

Inventing

YALE UNIVERSITY PRESS   NEW HAVEN & LONDON

a Nation

Washington,

Adams,

Jefferson

Gore Vidal

Designed by Rebecca Gibb. Set in Janson type
by Integrated Publishing Solutions,
Grand Rapids, Michigan. Printed
in the United States of America by
R. R. Donnelley, Harrisonburg, Virginia.

Library of Congress Cataloging-in-Publication Data
Vidal, Gore, 1925–
Inventing a nation : Washington, Adams, Jefferson / Gore Vidal
p. cm.
Includes index.
ISBN 0-300-10171-6 (alk. paper)
1. United States—Politics and government—1775–1783. 2. United States—
Politics and government—1783–1809. 3. Statesmen—United States—Biography.
4. Washington, George, 1732–1799. 5. Adams, John, 1735–1826. 6. Jefferson,
Thomas, 1743–1826. I. Title.
E302.1.V57 2003
973.4'092'2—dc22
2003015612

A catalogue record for this book is available from the British Library.

The paper in this book meets the guidelines for permanence and durability
of the Committee on Production Guidelines for Book Longevity
of the Council on Library Resources.

10 9 8 7 6 5 4 3 2 1

Inventing a Nation

~One~

In the fall of 1786 the fifty-four-year-old president of the Potomac Company, George Washington, late commander in chief of the American army (resigned December 23, 1783, after eight years of active duty) was seriously broke. Majestically, he had refused any salary from the revolutionary American government so seldom in useful Congress assembled. But it had always been agreed that should their cause be victorious, Congress would pay the General's expenses, which it did, with some awe at Washington's meticulous bookkeeping and lavish way of life—Congress had to cough up $100,000.

Now the General was retired to his Virginia plantation, Mount Vernon. Despite one hundred slaves, Mount Vernon yielded insufficient revenue, while various western lands on the Ohio River were costing the General more than they brought in. Worse, since he was the world's most famous man he was also the most visited at home by both countrymen and wide-eyed Europeans. He was an indulgent host; unfortunately, neither his wealth nor that of his wife, Martha Custis, could pay for so royal a way of life. At one point, he seriously considered retreating north to Niagara; if that did not keep his admirers at bay, he was willing to flee even farther into Canada in order to escape his expensive fame. But a few trips away from Mount Vernon made it clear that there was to be no escape for him anywhere; he was to be famous for life and, probably, for all he knew or suspected, thereafter. Glumly he wrote, "My living under the best economy I can use must unavoidably be expensive." Plainly, Mount Vernon was to be "a well-resorted tavern, [frequented by] any strangers who are going from North to South or from South to North." Yet his crops were sparse. Bad soil. Too little fertilizer. He needed to be, he complained, Midas-like, "one who can convert everything he touches into manure as the first transmutation towards gold."

Reluctantly (apparent reluctance was his style whenever something desirable came his way), Washington had accepted the presidency of a joint Virginia-Maryland company to develop the navigability of the Potomac River—the so-called River of Swans—upon whose bank sat Mount Vernon itself. In early 1785 Washington was offered valuable shares in the company for himself and his heirs. He accepted only with the proviso that he might give whatever dividends that came his way to charities. This letter of stern condition became, as intended, the most highly publicized part of the legislature's official grant. The ongoing, self-nurtured image of Washington as a modest and even selfless hero had made him for sixteen years the iconic—today's overused word—center of the world's stage. When word spread that he had refused the kingship of the newly founded American Union, an astonished King George III noted that if this story was true, "He will be the greatest man in the world." The story was, we are told, true; and so he was. Others felt that he had been tempted but for two things: for George III to be succeeded by George IV (or even I) had a slightly surreal, even retrogressive ring to it: finally, there was no heir, no Prince of Virginia plotting in Tidewater, prey to chiggers.

Before 1789 the thirteen former British colonies were held uneasily together by certain fraying Articles of Confederation. Like the squire of Mount Vernon, most of the States were now broke, and it seemed impossible for the weak Confederation to raise sufficient revenues to pay off the interest and principal of the debt incurred during eight years of war. What to do? On February 28, 1785, a worried Washington wrote the Confederation's secretary for war, Henry Knox, that in the absence of a serious federal government, "we are no more than a rope of sand, and shall as easily be broken." When fellow Southerners warned that a stronger Union would mean New England's "tyranny" over the South, Washington wrote, "If we are afraid to trust one another under qualified powers, there is an end of the Union."

The question pending was by whom and to what end were the powers of such a Confederation or Union to be qualified.

Washington knew that something would have to be done more soon than late to strengthen the Articles of Confederation: others agreed. Immediately, there was a division between those eager for a new centralized federal arrangement and those who wanted the States to be only loosely affiliated. The first group became known as Federalists; the second, as supporters of states' rights, were Anti-Federalists, later to be known as Republicans. The first were mostly men who had made their mark in the Revolution; they were young; they tended to be lawyers, a new aristocracy—at least that was how they were regarded in New York, Boston, and Philadelphia. The Republicans were often rural magnates like Patrick Henry of Virginia. Washington, the embodiment of Federalism, was also first among the rural magnates, while the author of the Declaration of Independence, the former governor of Virginia Thomas Jefferson, was—with his famous pursuit of happiness for all but slaves and other untidy human fractions—a focal point for future Republicanism. Happily for the Federalists, as of 1786 Jefferson was the Union's minister to France and so out of range unlike the thin-skinned Washington who, although above the political battle, nevertheless subscribed to ten newspapers not by any means friendly to the president of the Potomac Company, currently under attack for having spent fifteen guineas for a pair of French pheasants—a terrible unpatriotic waste of money. Actually, the birds were a present from Louis XVI, to be delivered by Washington's old friend and wartime colleague Lafayette. One can imagine a tabloid of today telling its readers, on page six, how fifteen American "peasants" had been bought by President Chirac.

On May 18, 1786, Washington wrote John Jay, "That it is necessary to revise and amend the Articles of Confederation, I entertain no doubt; but what may be the consequences of such an attempt is doubtful yet something must be done, or the fabric must fall, for it certainly is tottering." In September a meeting of representatives from the thirteen States was requested by Virginia to assemble at Annapolis, capital of Maryland. They were instructed to report on "the trade and commerce of the United States" and nothing more. But a New York delegate, the thirty-two-year-old lawyer Alexander Hamilton, arrived with a three-year-old draft of a constitution in his pocket. Unfortunately, and to Washington's dismay, only five state delegations showed up, less than a quorum. Undismayed, Hamilton kept busy. He allied himself with the other brilliant delegate, the thirty-five-year-old James Madison of Virginia. Madison and Hamilton were more or less as one for a strong federal government. But it was Madison who had fought in the Virginia legislature for interstate conventions, and now the one at Annapolis proved to be the key. Washington's anxiety was somewhat mitigated when twelve delegates, headed by Hamilton (Washington's former military aide), had taken it upon themselves to call for a second assembly to meet the second Monday of the following May, 1787, to review and revise the Articles of Confederation.

Meanwhile, the rickety Confederation was appalled when Massachusetts was revolutionized by one Captain Daniel Shays, a revolutionary hero whom Lafayette himself had presented with an expensive sword. But by September of 1786 Shays was obliged to sell the sword. Massachusetts was in a general depression. Worse, its Commonwealth taxes were more onerous than those so recently paid to the faraway King George. When new signs of rebellion in Rhode Island were reported, Madison, the future Republican, was now very much in Federalist mode. He wrote Jefferson in Paris: "Many gentlemen, both within and without Congress, wish to make this meeting subservient to a plenipotentiary Convention for amending the Confederation. Tho' my wishes are in favor of such an event, yet I despair so much of its accomplishment at the present crisis that I do not extend my views beyond a commercial reform."

Meanwhile, Captain Shays, having sold Lafayette's sword to feed his family, took up the terrible swift sword of revolution. With an army of veterans, he prepared to seize the national armory at Springfield. En route, jails were broken into and debtors freed. The rhetoric of the Shaysites was calculated to terrify the merchant class: "That the property of the United States has been protected from confiscation of Britain by the joint exertion of *all*, and ought to be the *common property* of all." In this crisis, there were no Federalists, no future Republicans: only frightened men of property. Most, by now, wanted to create a strong new nation where no revolt like that of Daniel Shays could ever again happen and where tranquillity, if not happiness, was the common pursuit.

In February 1787 Washington was officially notified that Congress, in response to the efforts of Hamilton and Madison, had named the second Monday in May for a convention to meet in Philadelphia "for the sole and express purpose of revising the Articles of Confederation." This was disingenuous. From the start of the famous Constitutional Convention, the prime movers, Hamilton and Madison, were actively engaged not in revising these (to them) inadequate articles but in replacing them: Washington's rope of sand was to be replaced by a supple chain of bronze.

Finally, New York State joined forces with those of Massachusetts to put down Shays's rebellion, which was now threatening to abolish all debts, divide up property, print paper money, and even reunite with England. "I am mortified beyond expression," Washington wrote "Light Horse" Harry Lee of Revolutionary fame, "when I view the clouds that have spread over the brightest morn that ever dawned upon any country." To the suggestion that his great influence should be invoked, Washington wrote, "In order to appease the present tumults in Massachusetts . . . I know not where that influence is to be found and, if attainable, that it would be a proper remedy for our disorders. . . . Influence is no government." Nevertheless, Shays's revolt was defeated by the Massachusetts militia February 2, 1787.

On November 5 Washington made his moves. He wrote to James Madison, now a member of the Virginia House of Delegates, "Without some alteration in our political creed, the superstructure we have been seven years raising at the expense of so much blood and treasure, must fall. We are fast verging to anarchy and confusion." But despite the best efforts of Madison and Hamilton, Congress would agree only to the Annapolis Convention's proposal that there be a meeting of delegates from all the States at Philadelphia in May "to take into consideration the Trade and Commerce of the United States." Hamilton's attempt to extend this narrow mandate was stopped by the Virginians. Madison had been for biding their time until . . . Washington's letter, which made all the difference. Madison could now enlist the country's greatest man as favoring, in the Annapolis Convention's phrase, "a general revision of the federal system." Building upon Washington's "some alteration in our political creed," Madison himself was, he wrote, "leaning to the side of hope." For one thing, the Virginia Assembly had voted for "general revision." It had also voted to send seven delegates to Philadelphia, led by General Washington.

Washington was reluctant, as always, to go. This time he had a new sort of excuse. He had been expected to attend the triennial meeting of the Society of the Cincinnati in May at Philadelphia. But due to rheumatism and long-neglected business affairs, he had said that he could not be present. The Society was made up of those officers who had served with him in the Revolution. It had also been founded as a hereditary affair of knightly men. For Jefferson it was too aristocratic by half. Washington agonized to his friends over the hurt feelings of the Cincinnati once they realized that he preferred making a new constitution to further bonding with them. Madison played the General delicately. Perhaps little Jemmy (five-foot-six) already understood that it was necessary for Big George (six-foot-three) to imitate such classical heroes as Cincinnatus himself, who, after winning victories for Rome, gave up his dictatorship and went home to raise cabbages in manly obscurity.

During this time of anguish, trapped between two sets of duty, Washington had a row with his mother, a woman as strong-minded as he. She asked him to send her fifteen guineas. He did so—reluctantly, as it was all the cash that he had on hand: "It is really hard upon me when you have taken everything you wanted from the plantation, by which money could be raised, when I have not received one farthing directly nor indirectly from the place for more than twelve years if ever, and when in that time, I have paid . . . (during my absence) two hundred and sixty odd pounds, and by my own account fifty odd pounds out of my own pocket to you, besides (if I am rightly informed) everything that has been raised by the crops on the plantation." Thus the father of his country to its unwitting grandmother.

As Washington—perhaps sensing that the biographer Parson

Weems would one day immortalize him as "the boy who could not tell a lie"—continued to fret about what the Cincinnati might think of him if they knew he had chosen to ignore them in order to birth a new nation. By mid-March, he said he would remain home, true to his word to them. Apparently, the rheumatism was indeed so bad that he could not turn over in bed without pain; he also wore one arm in a sling. Pressure to go to the Constitutional Convention came from Madison. From Knox, dire warnings that the convention without him would be as irrelevant as Annapolis. Simultaneously, Washington was worried about what his *non*-attendance might be attributed to. Antirepublicanism? Pro-monarchism? Finally, day after day, those ten newspapers reported to him that every state seemed to be sending its most illustrious sons. Yet had he not vowed, upon retirement, to never more "intermeddle in public matters"? How could the people ever again trust him if he . . . ?

On April 9 he crossed the Rubicon. He would go to the Constitutional Convention even though "under the peculiar circumstances of my case [it] would place me in a more disagreeable situation than any other member would stand in, as I have yielded, however, to what appeared to be the earnest wishes of my friends, I will hope for the best." Not a word about begetting a new exceptional nation where happiness would forever reign. Worse, Mother was seriously ill. He hurried to her home in Fredericksburg. Mother was better. He also visited one of his farms, and investigated a new method of growing potatoes. On May 9 he left for Philadelphia, unaccompanied by his wife, known to all of classless America as Lady Washington. Martha does not figure as greatly as Mother in Washington's archetypal life. A nephew was left in charge of Mount Vernon.

The General was made much of on his journey north. The millionaire banker Robert Morris insisted that Washington, "America's first millionaire," should stay with him at Fifth and Market streets.

"On my arrival," Washington noted in his diary, "the bells were chimed." On the other hand, to his annoyance, only the Virginia and Pennsylvania delegates had arrived by what was to have been the first day of the convention. Madison was soothing. Bad weather. Muddy roads. Persevere. By May 25, seven of the states' delegates, a quorum, were on hand, and the convention could organize itself, Washington was unanimously chosen to be president of the convention. He took his chair. The weather continued bad.

On Monday, September 17, 1787, the Committee on Style and Arrangement, presided over by one of the most active of the delegates to the convention, the elegant, eloquent, antidemocratic Gouverneur Morris of New York, presented the finished Constitution to the president of the Potomac Company. It is interesting that another New York delegate, Hamilton, had not stayed on through the hot Philadelphia summer. He had a greater task ahead. He would explain—that is, sell—the Constitution to the people in the coming months. The United States of America would become a republic ("if we can keep it," said Benjamin Franklin).

Governance was triune: a legislative branch composed of a Senate—two senators from each state—and a House of Representatives elected every two years by those men of property qualified to vote in the States. There was also a judiciary headed by a Supreme Court whose functions were not entirely clear. Finally, there was an executive branch whose chief would be called the president. Since the president was bound to be Washington, he was also commander in chief of the armed forces. Might not a future president overthrow the state with his military forces? In 1790 the army numbered less than seven hundred men; it was decided that the future must look to itself.

An amendment to reduce the majority required to override a presidential veto from three-fourths to two-thirds was voted down despite Washington's objection. The word *veto* did not appear in the text. Madison preferred the phrase *to negative*. Gouverneur Morris was highly critical of the style and arrangement of Article III, creating the Supreme Court, which he himself had written. "The Congress shall have power to declare the punishment of Treason, but no Attainder of Treason shall work Corruption of Blood or Forfeiture except during the Life of the Person attainted." Gnarled prose no doubt certain to be soon clarified by our twenty-first-century Court, in the pellucid prose, one prays, of that model associate justice Clarence Thomas.

At the last moment, three delegates would not sign the draft.

Each wanted to call a second convention but since upon reflection the whole thing might simply fall apart, the prime movers pledged that the Constitution, if accepted unanimously *now*, would be added to later ("engorged" was the verb). Thus, the old Articles of Confederation were replaced by an as yet *un*engorged Constitution, which is, to this day, often subject to *dis*engorgement, particularly of George Mason's original Bill of Rights. After all, Mason had written the state of Virginia's 1776 constitution whose "Declaration of Rights" contained the doctrine of "inalienable rights" (borrowed from John Locke) which Jefferson most famously made a cornerstone of his Declaration of Independence. Theoretically, if not practically, Mason also opposed the Constitution's implicit approval of slavery as well as its approval of the continuance of the slave trade for the next twenty years. Later, he opposed Virginia's ratification of the Washington-Madison-Hamilton (inspired if not by them blessed) Constitution. Then, once the republic was in place, he refused to serve as one of his state's senators. He has had few political heirs.

Madison had kept notes of the original convention debates. He also outlived the other framers, which meant that by the 1820s he was the last recognized authority on what the founders had in mind when they drafted that Constitution to which, in the First Congress of the new republic, ten amendments, the so-called Bill of Rights, were added. Although the language of amendments and constitutional articles are admirably plain, interested interpreters have often displayed great ingenuity in fiddling with their meaning. Whenever Madison was quizzed about "original intent," he had a stock answer: if you are really curious as to what the delegates had in mind, study the debates at the time of ratification. *Everything*, he felt, was argued out in the thirteen legislatures and what was originally meant is generally quite clear. Obviously, contemporary politics often have a blurring effect or, as Jefferson confessed, he—and others—were so concentrated for so long on the evils of monarchy that they came to believe that anything that was *not* monarchical was republican and so acceptable, which was nonsense. Although Jefferson was not a convention delegate, he later objected that the president was eligible to succeed himself without limit. He would have favored something like the later Twenty-second Amendment, which limits that magistrate to two terms. Jefferson also believed—uniquely—that this world belongs, solely, to the present generation. Hence, every twenty years or so, new laws should be promulgated at a constitutional convention. A grown man, he noted in his best biblical parable style, should not be forced to wear a boy's jacket. With characteristic tact, James Madison, who had plainly found one constitutional convention quite enough for a single lifetime, pointed out the impossibility of achieving a viable republic if its laws were to be periodically set aside in favor of new ones. In fact, so disturbed was he by Jefferson's metaphysical—even existential—notions that he made the case against too frequent conventions in the Federalist papers.

Federalist No. 49 is attributed to Madison, although Hamilton later claimed it was his handiwork. The essay strikes this reader as a continuation—even summing up—of Madison versus Jefferson on too frequent constitutional conventions. Demurely, Madison praises his fellow Virginian. Then, "One of the precautions which he [Jefferson] proposes, and on which he appears ultimately to rely as a palladium to the weaker departments of power against the invasion of the stronger, is perhaps altogether his own . . . "—for Madison, in such matters originality is invariably suspect—" . . . and as it immediately relates to the subject of our present inquiry, ought not to be overlooked. His proposition is that whenever any two of the three branches of government shall concur in opinion, each by the voices of two-thirds of their whole number, that a convention is necessary for altering the constitution, *or correcting breaches of it,* a convention shall be called for the purpose." The author of 49, at this point, adverts to David Hume. "If it be true that all governments rest on opinion, it is no less true that the strength of opinion in each individual, and its practical influence on his conduct, depend much on the number which he supposes to have entertained the same opinion. The reason of man, like man himself, is timid and cautious when left alone, and acquires firmness and confidence in proportion to the number with which it is associated."

In the next essay, Federalist No. 50, currently attributed to

Madison, one hears, oddly, more the energetic voice of Hamilton, while in No. 51 one gets such Hamiltonian locutions as "Ambition must be made to counteract ambition." In fact, this might be his philosophy of republican government in a phrase. "The interest of the man must be connected with the constitutional rights of the place. It may be a reflection on human nature, that such devices should be necessary to control the abuses of government. But what is government itself, but the greatest of all reflections on human nature? If men were angels, no government would be necessary. If angels were to govern men, neither external nor internal controls on government would be necessary." Then a—pious?—generality: "Justice is the end of government. It is the end of civil society. It has ever been and ever will be pursued until it be obtained, or until liberty be lost in the pursuit." This is also reflective of Sir James Steuart, in the previous generation. "The best way to govern a society, and to engage everyone to conduct himself according to a plan, is for the statesmen to run a system of administration the most consistent possible with the interest of every individual, and never flatter himself that his people will be brought to act . . . from any other principle than private interest."

Although Alexander Hamilton was a born political theorist, he played little part in the great business at Philadelphia. Since each state voted as a single unit and since, within his state delegation, he was outvoted by the Anti-Federalist interest, he spent much of his time back home in New York City, where he practiced law when not attending court at Albany. He would bide his time.

John Adams referred unkindly to Hamilton as "the bastard brat of a Scotch peddler," while even the Godlike Jefferson called him "base-born." Plainly speaking, both men were accurate. Rachel Fawcett, Alexander's mother, was married not to his father but to another. Everything else is confused, including the year of his birth. He thought it was 1757. Other "evidence" points to 1755— on the island of Nevis in the Lesser Antilles. James Hamilton of Ayrshire in Scotland fathered two sons with Rachel, who had been married, according to Alexander's grandson, to John Lavien, "a rich Danish Jew . . . who treated her cruelly." Rachel, a beauty, had numerous affairs with other men and, in due course, Lavien divorced her. Although Alexander resembled his putative father James—an athletic redhead—it was also rumored in that most scandalous of centuries, the twentieth, that his actual father was the twenty-three-year-old George Washington, who was traveling among the West Indian islands at the time of his conception. Other rumors declared that he was Lavien's son. Finally, thanks to Hamilton's dedication to the abolition of slavery, he was declared to be of black descent. In any case, it can be safely said that of the national founders he was the one true exotic.

When Alexander was thirteen, Rachel died. A year earlier the pubescent Hamilton had gone to work for two young New York bachelors, David Beckman or Beekman and Nicholas Cruger, who kept a store in St. Croix. The boy Hamilton was a brilliant bookkeeper and manager. He was also involved in the partners' traffic in African slaves and local mules. In 1769 he wrote a friend, "My ambition is prevalent. . . . I contemn the grov'ling condition of a clerk to which my fortune contemns me and would willingly risk my life tho' not my character to exalt my station." He also wrote, "I wish there was a war." He had read Plutarch. He knew how swiftly one could rise in war. And he *must* rise. Then his employers exalted his station. He was sent, at seventeen, to King's College (now Columbia) in New York City. He promptly joined in the debate over the colonies' secession from England. Then he helped organize a company to fight in the Revolution, risking life but not character. He so impressed Washington that the General chose him as aide-de-camp and private secretary, treating him as the son he was never to have, assuming Alexander was *not* his son. By 1789 Hamilton had become a lawyer; he had also married into the wealthy Schuyler family. Unlike the Virginians, he was seldom seriously broke.

It would appear that the principal fact of Hamilton's life was his illegitimacy and then orphanhood at thirteen. In a sense, he was something of a professional orphan, instinctively using his intellectual and personal charms to enchant potential protectors. Already, at thirteen, he was a precociously competent man of business. Later, he proved to be exactly what a childless middle-aged man of a slow cautious nature would want in an aide or secretary. Since Hamilton always tended to go to the top of whatever tree confronted him, he bedazzled the commanding general of the American army as he had charmed the two bachelors in St. Croix, as well as the island priest, the Reverend Hugh Knox, who gave him letters of introduction to New York worthies. But what did Hamilton see in Washington other than the demonstrable fact that he had been chosen commander in chief largely because, as John Adams sourly put it, "He was always the tallest man in the room."

Washington's gifts were not immediately evident. He seemed unable to win battles, not that he had much help from troops always ready to desert, or from the corrupt Continental Congress that kept him ill-supplied. "On our side," he wrote Congress in September 1776, "the wars should be defensive." He had little choice. He was in constant retreat, which annoyed his glory-hunting aide. But Washington was winning in his own way. If he could hold together his army long enough, the British would tire and go home. In the end, only Washington's majestic presence kept the army together. He was also lucky in his British counterparts: mediocrities to a man. (One British observer noted, "Any general in the world other than General Howe would have beaten General Washington; and any general in the world other than General Washington would have beaten General Howe.") Finally, the French fleet came to Washington's aid at Yorktown, and that was the end of that revolution. Although the British still held New York and other attractive properties, they eventually went home, as Washington had known they would.

By Yorktown, young Hamilton had distinguished himself in the field. After a row with Washington, who had accused him of keeping him waiting at the top of a flight of stairs, Hamilton quit as aide and went to war. Washington was duly shaken. Of this rupture, Hamilton wrote his father-in-law, the wealthy political magnate Philip Schuyler, "I always disliked the relation of an aide-de-camp to his general, as having in it a kind of personal dependence." Plainly, Hamilton was maturing. He was tired of being a childless man's bright little boy. But when he saw what he wrote, he crossed out *relation* and substituted *office*, then he cut the phrase *to his general*. He continues: "For three years past I have felt no friendship for him and professed none. The truth is our own dispositions are the opposites of each other, and the pride of my temper . . . could not suffer me to profess what I did not feel." Of Washington's invitation to a "candid conversation" Hamilton writes, "When advances of this kind have been made to me by the General, they were received in a manner that showed at least I had had no inclination to court them, and that I wished to stand rather upon a footing of military confidence than of private attachment." This is powerful stuff—indeed, this is classical playwriting at its best—and had the United States ever developed a true civilization (cellophane and Kleenex were never quite enough), our very own Racine would have known how to tell this story of Ganymede wanting to play Zeus, with the added excitement for the audience that, unknown to Ganymede, Zeus is his father. Well, why ask for the moon, as the heroine of a great film said, when we have the stars—not to mention all those stripes?

On September 17, 1787, the Constitution was sent to the thirteen States to be ratified. In New York a special convention was held at Poughkeepsie; and Hamilton was there to ensure its ratification despite the Republican element, led by the state's governor George Clinton. When Hamilton promptly, characteristically, went on the attack, Washington warned him off. They needed the powerful Clinton for their republic. Meanwhile, Hamilton decided to write a series of essays, anticipating objections. He would, as was the custom then, publish pseudonymously in newspapers. The first essay was signed "A Citizen of New York." He envisaged around twenty essays with the overall title *The Federalist*. But by the time the first was published, October 27, 1787, he knew that he would need help. Not since Machiavelli had so ambitious and thorough a system been conceived as the apparent work of a single intelligence.

Hamilton turned to John Jay, who agreed to help. Jay had not been in Philadelphia, but he was knowledgeable in foreign affairs. Hamilton then approached Gouverneur Morris, an inspired notion, but Morris had business to do in Virginia. Hamilton then turned to James Madison, whose notes must have been of great use to the enterprise. "A Citizen of New York" took early retirement, and "Publius" took his place. The joint use of the name of Publius Valerius was certainly calculated to please Jefferson and even Clinton. After the expulsion of the Tarquin kings from

Rome, Publius Valerius had helped create the Roman Republic. He was then chosen as one of the first two consuls. When his co-consul died, it was rumored that Publius would make himself king. To prove that he was no monarchist, he promulgated a law that anyone attempting to make himself king could be slain with impunity by any citizen. Publius's nickname was Publicola— "friend of the people."

"Publius's" main task was one of definition. Today's political babble seems to believe that *democracy* and *republic* are synonyms. They are not. As Publius tried to make clear, they were as much polar opposites as monarchy and democracy. For the founders, democracy meant Athens, where all the citizens would meet to discuss and pass on the laws. The voice of the people was indeed god. This was possible in a small city-state like Athens but impractical in a large nation of three million people ever expanding over a large area of North America. It is seldom noted that in 1776 every fourth Englishman was an American. Had England allowed Americans to elect members of Parliament, annulling the cry "no taxation without representation," there might have been no revolution. But in the end, geography decided the matter. Between election and a transatlantic journey, the American member of Parliament would always be too far from home to represent home. So now home was to have its very own government in the form of a three-part republic, so carefully checked and balanced that no Caesar, much less mob, could easily hijack it.

Some historians looking back on the making of the republic refer to "the great collaboration," meaning Jefferson and Madison. But the actual collaboration was between Madison and Hamilton during the period when the Constitution was up for ratification. There was also an ongoing collaboration between the squire of Mount Vernon and his former secretary-aide, Hamilton. Washington then posed as a passive eminence, worrying about his debts and new ways of growing potatoes (in fields of clover), he was using Hamilton (and Madison) to shape events to his liking.

Washington-Hamilton. Now that we are safely lodged in the twenty-first century, the New Age of the last unlamented century behind us, we need not do in-depth readings of those we know of only through fame's glare, which simultaneously illuminates and blurs.

Although the hostile "Republican" Governor Clinton presided over the convention, Hamilton was well known to the delegates as "Publius," coauthor with Madison of eighty-five essays (Jay wrote five) published in two volumes called *The Federalist*. He led the debate for the Feds. Melancton Smith for the Antis. Smith thought the Constitution favored too much "the natural aristocracy" rather than "the middling classes." Hamilton promptly raised, as it were, the ante: "In free . . . republics the will of the people makes the essential principle of the government; and the laws which control the community receive their tone and spirit from the public wishes. It is the fortunate situation of our country, that the minds of the people are exceedingly enlightened and refined." This took the wind out of the Antis' sails. It was the later Federalist Hamilton who noted that "your people, sir, is a great beast." Now he carefully circled the subject. All agreed that the ancient democracies were easily swayed by the demagogue, while "the true principle of a republic is, that the people should choose whom they please to govern them." Finally, Hamilton's great proposition—how to use human greed and energy—(*energy* was a favorite word that energetic season)—to serve the state. "Men will pursue their interests . . . it is as easy to change human nature as to oppose the strong current of selfish passions. A wise legislator will gently divert the channel and direct it, if possible, to the public good." Incidentally, true Hamiltonians like Stephen F. Knott (*Alexander Hamilton and the Persistence of Myth*, University Press of Kansas, 2002) cannot trace Hamilton's beastly view of the people to any reliable source. Knott makes the case that Hamilton always favored representative government with checks and balances to contain "majority tyranny" in which he resembled Jefferson.

Then, dramatically, word came to the delegates that New Hampshire had ratified the Constitution, the ninth state to do so. A quorum had been attained: the Republic of the United States was a fact. But New York and Virginia had still not ratified. An Anti-Fed promptly announced that since nine states had endorsed the Constitution, let them go try the experiment on their own. New York would stay put. On July 2, while Clinton was in midspeech, a messenger arrived with a letter from Madison to Hamilton: Virginia had ratified. Despite Federalist cheers, Clinton continued to delay ratification. Then word came from New York City that all the bells were ringing, and the city's leaders were threatening that should upstate delay ratification, the city—the state's wealth—would secede and join the new Union. On July 23 Melancton Smith gave in. New York State ratified. There was much celebrating in New York City, the capital of the new nation. A parade featuring a ship called *The Hamilton*, on a float, sailed triumphantly along Wall Street as its ghost still does today. This was to be the high point in the life of the "bastard brat" from the West Indies.

Two

It is safe to assume that no work of a committee has ever given quite the same pleasure to each member of that committee. The Constitution of 1787 pleased some of its authors more than others, while neither of the two prime progenitors (godfathers one might say), John Adams of Massachusetts and Thomas Jefferson of Virginia, had been a delegate to the Constitutional Convention. But a decade earlier, in the summer of 1776, Jefferson had been at Philadelphia as a dutiful if reluctant member of the Continental Congress—reluctant in the sense that he would have much preferred to be at his state's capital, Williamsburg, working on a draft constitution for the Commonwealth of Virginia, recently separated from England. Instead of Jefferson it was George Mason who, on May 27, 1776, completed a draft of a sternly conservative instrument for the governance of Virginia despite the radical underlying premise that "all men are born free and independent and have certain inherent natural rights . . . among which are the enjoyment of life and liberty, with the means of acquiring and possessing property and pursuing and obtaining happiness and safety."

Later that most famous summer of 1776, Jefferson wrote the Declaration of Independence, making literature of Mason's somewhat desultory laundry list, consisting of John Locke's garments. Also, on his own, Jefferson produced three drafts of a constitution for Virginia. Meanwhile, throughout the thirteen former British colonies, Jefferson's Declaration was circulated to a people in rebellion as well as to those still loyal to the British Crown: "We hold these truths to be sacred & undeniable [Jefferson's original version]; that all men are created equal & independant, that from that equal creation they derive rights inherent & inalienable, among which are the preservation of life, & liberty, & the pursuit of happiness." Congress, in its editing, introduced a Creator. Astonishingly, John Locke's *property* was suddenly out the window, thanks to Jefferson, who had substituted "the pursuit of happiness," something new under the political sun.

The conservative Mason had also, in effect, shrunk the already minuscule roster of those white men of property who could vote directly for members of Congress and various state officials. Mason's guidelines would have allowed only a miniscule percentage of the population to vote, thus keeping control of the government in the hands of the slave-owning planters. Jefferson, though a member of the ruling oligarchy, kept the property-owning proviso but then, ingeniously, argued that any white man with a fifty-acre freehold could vote while those, otherwise qualified, who lacked the necessary acreage would be granted free land by the state, thus extending the total propertied franchise to thousands of new voters. Jefferson's distaste for monarchy was notorious: less remarked upon was his edgy dislike of the aristocracy to which he belonged as a member of the slave-owning class.

John Adams, something of an expert with the needle, often enjoyed using it on the sometimes self-righteous Jefferson. Although neither was happy with the way that the office of president had been established in the Constitution, Jefferson felt that it was a mistake to allow a president the right to keep on succeeding himself like "a bad edition of a Polish king." Adams, who tended to admire the British arrangements of an elected representative parliament in tandem with an hereditary monarch, aroused deep mistrust in Jefferson who saw in Adams a pro- or cryptomonarchist. Yet Adams admitted in a letter to Jefferson that "I find it difficult to reconcile myself to the notion of multiple terms for a president. We agree perfectly that the many should have a full fair and perfect representation." The House of Representatives—with its election of all members every two years—was as close to actual democracy as the founders were ever to get. But in the second chamber the Senators were chosen not by the people but by the legislatures of the States; this struck

Adams as protoaristocratical. Adams, very much aware of Jefferson's doubts about Adams's own loyalty to Demos, wrote his then friend and later enemy (and, finally, friend again, as each in his final years withdrew farther and farther up the slopes of Mount Olympus, where George Washington had preceded them; happily, the Disney-like Mount Rushmore was as yet a nightmare undreamed of by either patriot): "You are apprehensive of monarchy, I of aristocracy. I would therefore have given more power to the President and less to the Senate."

As it proved, both Jefferson and Adams publicly endorsed the Constitution, each with fingers crossed; each confident that one day, more soon than late, there would be another convention and what proved faulty could be corrected. Neither was as prescient, even as harsh, as was America's great universal man—publisher, author, diplomat, inventor Benjamin Franklin in his endorsement [*sic*?] of the 1787 instrument, forged in his hometown of Philadelphia.

At eighty-one Franklin was too feeble to address the convention on its handiwork, and so a friend read for him the following words: "I agree to this Constitution with all its faults, if they are such: because I think a General Government necessary for us, and there is no *Form* of Government but what may be a Blessing to the People if well-administred; and I believe farther that this is likely to be well administred for a Course of Years and can only end in Despotism as other Forms have done before it, when the

People shall become so corrupted as to need Despotic Government, being incapable of any other."

Now, two centuries and sixteen years later, Franklin's blunt dark prophecy has come true: popular corruption has indeed given birth to that Despotic Government which he foresaw as inevitable at our birth. Unsurprisingly, a third edition of the admirable *Benjamin Franklin: His Life As He Wrote It*, by Esmond Wright, is now on sale (Harvard University Press, 1996) with, significantly—inevitably?, Franklin's somber prediction cut out, thus silencing our only great ancestral voice to predict Enron *et seq.*, not to mention November 2000, and, following that, despotism whose traditional activity, war, now hedges us all around. No wonder that so many academic histories of our republic and its origins tend to gaze fixedly upon the sunny aspects of a history growing ever darker. No wonder they choose to disregard the wise, eerily prescient voice of the authentic Franklin in favor of the jolly fat ventriloquist of common lore, with his simple maxims for simple folk; to ignore his key to our earthly political invention in favor of that lesser key which he attached to a kite in order to attract heavenly fire.

In the New England schooldays of the present writer, it was thought a good idea for the history class to memorize the Declaration of Independence. Yet he no longer recalls—was not encouraged to dwell on?—the lines that followed "Pursuit of Happiness." The very next sentence reads: "That to secure these rights,

Governments are instituted among Men, deriving their just powers from the consent of the governed." Good stuff. But not even Franklin could have foreseen today's never-ending corporate funded elections entirely devoid of actual politics, while we can only guess what Jefferson, during one of his periodic readjustments of the Constitution, would have done with the ultimate constitutional arbiter of our popular elections, the Electoral College, which consists not of the people but of their rulers' surrogates. At this point in Jefferson's enthusiastic original prose, there is a total—intended?—blank in one schoolboy's memory. "That whenever any Form of Government becomes destructive of these ends, it is the right of the People to alter or abolish it." Back in the forties we must have thought that this referred only to the odious tyranny of King George III, and not to any future breakdown in our ongoing arrangements as we invented what we assumed would be ever more perfect unions.

But Jefferson did anticipate part of Franklin's demur. After all, what the people have made they can unmake. From the beginning, Jefferson wanted a new constitutional convention every twenty years or so, while Franklin himself went boldly on record with the prediction that our people would drift into so deep a corruption that only despots could rule them. It is impossible that Jefferson and Franklin did not discuss so great a matter. What was said? It would appear that even to this day Franklin has been censored. In the best of America's high school history books, *The American Pageant*, by Kennedy, Cohen, and Bailey

(Houghton Mifflin, 2002), there is a curious passage about Franklin vis-à-vis the Constitutional Convention: Franklin "was inclined to be indiscreetly talkative in his declining years. Concerned for the secrecy of their deliberations, the convention assigned chaperones to accompany Franklin to dinner parties and make sure he held his tongue." Thus were we deprived of the wisdom of the only worldly—not to mention perhaps the wisest—of the founders. But then much in our intellectual-political life has always been ritually suppressed for secrecy's sake.

Although it is hardly conceivable for any American now alive to imagine the "Revolution" as never having taken place, there is very little about the events of 1776 that, on close examination, suggests inevitability. The "better elements" were more or less content with the status quo. The middling, mercantile classes objected to being taxed by a far-off government at London. Those who read pamphlets—and history—were intrigued by the anomaly of so small and distant an island governing the better part of a continent. Worse, the weird arrangement of a German crown tacked onto an insular British Parliament led to all sorts of irritable party infighting, much of it irrelevant to the residents of the American colonies. To American complaints that they paid taxes to support the British empire from which they got nothing back, the British loftily answered that British arms alone had saved the colonists from the predatory French in Canada and the murderous Indians (often allied with France) who together had posed a constant threat.

Finally, the first move toward the creation of a new republic was not so much to rid the colonists of their British masters as to intimidate disaffected American veterans of the various tax rebellions that preceded the step-by-idle-step establishment of the United States of America. One of these early steps entered the new nation's permanent folklore when Bostonians underscored their refusal to pay a 1773 tax on tea by dumping the tea in Boston harbor. Coincidentally, a more than usually dim government at London, eager to raise revenue to pay for their Seven Years' War with France, was inspired to impose a government stamp to prove that a vendor had paid tax to the crown. This was the beginning of the end of the British adventure in North America; 1775 proved to be a year of rebellion here and there as well as of conciliation, more here than there. John Adams, looking back from the vantage point of 1818, was inspired to remark: "The Revolution was effected before the war commenced. The Revolution was in the minds and hearts of the people."

As British troops had occupied Boston since 1768, it should have been an easy matter to unmask those fun-loving Bostonians (some disguised as Indians) who celebrated the Yuletide season by dumping imported British tea into Boston harbor. The British responded to this revolutionary act with uncharacteristic subtlety. Hard-faced businessmen in London were quick to realize that the powerhouse of their economy, the East India Company, was suddenly stuck with several million pounds of unsold tea and no American market. The company was encouraged to sell the tea at close to cost, inclusive, however—as salt on the wound—of a three-pence tax, the object of the imperial exercise. Principle triumphed until the colonists united sufficiently to ship all the tea home to England. There Parliament, in its wrath, inflicted a series of Intolerable Acts upon the colonists, among them restricting the sacred New England town meetings while ensuring that any Briton driven to murder by an intolerable American must be sent home to England for a "fair trial." Suddenly, "no taxation without representation" dominated the political debate, and the thirteen often politically indolent entities now acted as if Dr. Franklin's electrified key had sprung some secret lock in their constituent beings.

On September 5, 1774, forty-five of the weightiest colonial men formed the First Continental Congress at Philadelphia. The weightiest of the lot was the Boston lawyer John Adams, known as the best-read man in Boston. Short, fat, given to bouts of vanity that alternated with its first cousin self-pity, he was thirty-nine years old when he joined the Massachusetts delegation to the Congress. He was married to Abigail Smith, a marriage somewhat similar to that of his father, John the farmer, to Susanna Boylston. Each Adams had seemed instinctively to be obeying an old law of new societies, by marrying above his social station: farmer John to a Boylston, while Abigail's mother was a storied Quincy.

The one who moves up is known as a hypergamist and, not too surprisingly, such marriages tend to be happier than classic love matches between like-stationed couples. Certainly, Abigail and John were the most interesting couple among the founders of the embryo nation, and their letters to each other are still a joy to read; nor were they alone in their marital adventurousness; even the protocolossus, Washington, had condescended to marry a grand fortune.

If Adams was the loftiest of the scholars at the Continental Congress of 1775, Thomas Jefferson was the most intricate character, gifted as writer, architect, farmer—and, in a corrupt moment, he allowed his cook to give birth to that unique dessert later known as Baked Alaska. Like Adams, he had tried his hand at constitution making in the spring of 1776. He sent *A Summary View of the Rights of British America* to Patrick Henry, the orator and professional Virginia politician, but got no answer. Henry reputedly had a problem with laudanum, the drug of the day. Jefferson was not pleased with this rebuff: "Whether Mr. Henry disapproved the ground taken," he later wrote, "or was too lazy to read it (for he was the laziest man in reading I ever knew) I never learned but he communicated it to nobody."

From April 1775 to July 1776 the undeclared war between England and its American colonies smoldered; flared up; appeared to sputter out . . . It was hardly, ever, a mass rebellion. For one thing, sixteen percent of the Americans were Tories: that is, loyalists to the crown. They were also among the wealthiest and best-educated of the colonists. Over the next eight years, as rebellion became war, many of them fled to Canada or even "back" to England, giving the radical lawyers who had taken charge of the Revolution a lucrative practice settling scores, not to mention estates.

The Second Continental Congress met on May 10, 1775, in a whole world, as the popular song had it, "turned upside down." A month before the Congress assembled, British troops fired, at Lexington in Massachusetts, on some American armed "minute men." Although eight Americans were killed, the British discovered to their no doubt horror, that American farmers and backwoodsmen *did not fight fair.* Instead of wearing bright red uniforms, visible for miles around, they tended to hide behind trees, bushes, rocks and, if nothing else, America was extraordinarily rich in these rustic objects. Where British soldiers strutted into battle in well-drilled ranks, the Americans slouched from bush to protecting wall and then, invisibly, fired at will. They were like . . . well, no other word for it, *INDIANS.* This sickening discovery was swiftly relayed back to London. King George III, who had made the monumental mistake of learning English, was very much the head of the war party, and so, more in anger than in sorrow, he dropped the mask of Mr. Nice Guy. He would now use *his* Indians, some thirty thousand German soldiers, mostly from Hesse, a Rhineland province bordering his family's Hanoverian place of origin. The Hessians turned out to be more generally effective than the American or, indeed, the British troops. They were also considered uncommonly attractive by American girls, who found the homegrown lads a bit on the scrawny, sallow side, later to be caricatured as "Uncle Sam." By the end of the Revolution, a great many Hessians had married American girls and settled down as contented farmers in the German sections of Pennsylvania and Delaware, their lubricious descendants to this day magically peopling the novels of Mr. John Updike.

Meanwhile, back in Philadelphia, John Adams had made the union between the two great revolutionary states, Massachusetts and Virginia, by pushing for the selection of the Virginian George Washington as commander of the American army. Washington's steady presence and regal confidence more than compensated for his poor performance in the field against British generals, themselves every bit as striking in their mediocrity as he. Congress chose to ignore the fact that Colonel Washington's one campaign against the French during the Seven Years' War ended with his capture by the French—who were, nevertheless, so impressed by his dignity (and height) that they gave him an escort from Pittsburgh back to his home on the Potomac.

As important that season as the selection of Washington as commanding general was the publication of Thomas Paine's *Common Sense* (1776). Paine, a corsetmaker's apprentice in London, had emigrated to America in 1774. A born writer whose prose caused John Adams to writhe with envy, Paine rode the whirlwind that was now sweeping through the colonies.

The government of Lord North at London, egged on by a periodically mad king, had taken to burning such American towns as Norfolk, Virginia, and Falmouth, Massachusetts, while the arrival of the sturdy Hessian lads who were destined to fulfill the dreams of so many nubile American girls only gave fits to their fathers and brothers. Now, Paine, in words of flame, told his new countrymen that it was time to get their act together. The king was and would never be a friend to the Americans. He should be regarded as what he was, "the royal Brute of Great Britain." Paine grasped this nettle monarchy, and from it he plucked this flower, Republic, the only form of government suitable to the genius of a people heterogeneous in background and yet alike in their condition as free men in a rich country available to all who were willing to deal firmly with the sometimes irritable indigenous population.

An American historian was asked what the United States response should have been to the suicide bombers who attacked New York City and the Pentagon in 2001. "Traditionally," he said, "such an assault should have been followed by an immediate invasion of Canada." This sensible response caused bewilderment in the United States of Amnesia. What on earth did Canada have to do with the recent gruesome attack? Answer: as little, certainly, as Afghanistan, which we then proceeded to pound to pieces. But . . . Canada?

In the autumn of 1775, British troops burned down what is now Portland, Maine. A somewhat ad hoc American army under former British general Richard Montgomery, instead of trying to retake Boston from the British, opted for a two-pronged invasion of Canada in order to add that vast chunk of real estate to our already large continental empire. Politically, if not militarily, this attempt at annexation was misguided. It was mistakenly assumed that Catholic French Quebec, now part of the Protestant British empire, would be eager to join our Confederation. The French Canadians had other plans. Montgomery's forces were beaten back. At Quebec, Montgomery's army was joined by the other prong to the attack, commanded by the brilliant, if bad-tempered general, Benedict Arnold. Later Arnold would loom large in American history as the man who twice turned his coat: once to the "patriotic" American cause; then back to the British side, for which he was denounced as a traitor even though, as yet, there was no nation for him to betray. But, originally, he had renounced allegiance to the king to take part in the overture to the Revolution. Ill-used, he felt, by his fellow turncoats he switched back to the British side and sold them the Hudson River fort at West Point for £6,300 and a commission in the British army. But his plan was detected. New York State kept West Point and the British army got Benedict Arnold. Meanwhile, the legendary "boy hero" of Quebec, who had carried the large dead body of General Montgomery from the field, went home to New York, to the law, to the political club Tammany Hall, which, in 1800, helped elect Thomas Jefferson third U.S. president, with himself, Aaron Burr, as vice president.

Despite a good deal of muddled military activity during 1775, there was no coherent political movement for independence, much less for the establishment of a republic like glorious Athens or imperial Rome. Happily for the cause of Freedom, British pyromania literally added fuel to the flame. A month after Quebec, the British set afire Norfolk, Virginia, inspiring the Bostonians to force the British to evacuate Boston in favor of New York, a far more congenial city filled with Tories of the best society. General Washington never reoccupied the city until the war was finally over and the British in their desultory way went, gradually, home. But first they greased the flagpole up which the American standard bearer shinnied before responding to the tug of gravity with a crash.

Three

In recent years when our one-time progenitress, England, underwent a political transformation late in life, the Conservative Party, after its exuberant fling with Margaret Thatcher, ceded all parliamentary power not to Labour but to something called New Labour. Its inventor, a young politician called Tony Blair, created an unprecedented parliamentary majority and what appeared to be a new sort of politics. All this, of course, is far in the future, but as we brood upon the political life of the United States at its beginning, a key to our original situation has been recently revealed by the current Crown-in-Parliament's leader, Mr. Blair.

An old Labour politician who disapproved of New Labour condemned the concept and blamed Blair for "having taken the politics out of politics." The politician was rapidly translated

from Commons to Lords as the new regime began. The old Labour politician was then summoned to Downing Street shortly
after Mr. Blair moved in. The meeting was surprisingly amiable.
Mr. Blair had only one complaint: "I'm not the one who took
the politics out of politics as you wrote. I was simply the first
Labour politician to note that the politics had already been taken
out of politics and that a traditional old-line party like Labour
was not possible when over sixty percent of the electorate con-
siders itself, rightly or wrongly, middle class."

There followed an astute analysis of the nature of political
parties in a republic, crowned or not. In short, one cannot have
a viable party of any kind that is not based upon the interests of
a class. The factory workers, miners, and other manual laborers
that constituted the classic British Labour Party had now, many
of them, gone to work in services, leaving their old jobs to auto-
mation or, perhaps ominously, cheap third-world workers. Aware
that his party's constituency had withered away except for a few
old romantics adrift in the fin de siècle consumer/advertiser
world, Blair presented himself as a practical nonideological tech-
nician with a soothing TV-side manner. Real issues were dodged
for as long as possible: whether or not the British currency should
be absorbed into the collective euro could be kept on hold for
quite some time. But the imperial American alliance was an un-
foreseen source of danger as yet unresolved.

What then, is the point to leaping more than two centuries
ahead of the story of the founding of the American republic?

Because Anglophone republicans are more alike than not; they are rooted in Magna Carta, common law, the unwritten British constitution, and the written, if much amended, American one. Each nation made its fortune as a maritime power; each tended to imperial expansion; each filled up as much of the world as possible until, finally, the second law of thermodynamics (everything is running down) began to apply itself, altering, at first gradually, and now more swiftly, the nature of two republics whose political arrangements once intended to afford their citizens the means to pursue a degree of material happiness are now drawing to a close as the corruption Franklin predicted has become institutionalized in the American republic-empire, whose despotism, in the name of homeland security, grounded upon the anticonstitutional USA Patriot Act of 2001 and its successor now at hand. Was this always implicit in our origins? The current example of the nation that gave us birth is a bit like a movie trailer of coming attractions.

Thomas Paine was hardly an inevitable figure, but there he was when needed, to admonish us to free ourselves of a corrupt monarchical system which, paradoxically, was, in most things, to be our political model. Franklin, who thought more deeply than any other well-recorded American, saw much of what was to come.

Franklin was often in Europe as an agent for the new American republic. With John Jay and John Adams, he handled the American end of a surprisingly generous-spirited peace treaty with England in November 1782. He also indulged in an inter-

esting diagnosis of what he took to be the British problem that
had forced their American colonies into a rebellion that led to
a republic more overt than England's. On March 17, 1783, he
wrote, in prophetic mode, to his friend Bishop Shipley:

> America will, with God's blessing, become a great and
> happy country; and England, if she has at length gained
> wisdom, will have gained something more valuable, and
> more essential to her prosperity, than all she has lost;
> and will still be a great and respectable nation. Her great
> disease at present is the numerous and enormous salaries
> and emoluments of office. Avarice and ambition are strong
> passions and, separately, act with great force on the human
> mind; but when both are united, and may be gratified in
> the same object, their violence is almost irresistible, and
> they hurry men headlong into factions and contentions,
> destructive of all good government. As long, therefore,
> as these great emoluments subsist, your Parliament will
> be a stormy sea, and your public councils confounded by
> private interests. But it requires much public spirit and
> virtue to abolish them; more than perhaps can now be
> found in a nation so long corrupted.

Thus Franklin, describing the England of 1783, nicely describes
the United States of 2003, a once "great and happy country"
being torn apart by avarice and ambition while our "public coun-
cils [are] confounded by private interests."

In 1781 the thirteen colonies bound themselves together with a written constitution called the Articles of Confederation, a document that can be read as blueprint for a state with no politics at all or, turned upside down, a free-for-all for what, in a later century, the American Augustus, Franklin Roosevelt, cigarette holder (if not tongue) in cheek, solemnly dubbed "the age of the common man" while his populist nemesis, Senator Huey Long, went far beyond him with his "share our wealth" program and his slogan "every man a king." The seeds that later bloomed in Roosevelt and Long were first planted by Daniel Shays and Jefferson. Ironically, as it turned out, Roosevelt, the most uncommon man of all, became a wartime dictator who created the American global empire while Huey Long, more dangerous than Shays to men of property, was gunned down by the usual lone mad assassin who so often recurs in American political life.

Postwar, the country under Truman (Tiberius? Too much?) and his secretary of state, the brilliant empire builder Dean Acheson, assembled and militarized that American state in which we uneasily dwell. But centuries ago we individuals were often so political as to be apolitical, with parties based less on class interests than on Plutarchian ambition. Also, unlike England, the United States had no capital city and, of course, no phantom crown to bow to. The seat of government was a ramshackle affair as the Continental Congress moved nervously from Philadelphia to New York City, with a later detour, during 1789, to Annapolis, Maryland. The most solemn of the founders deplored party faction on the British model: where England had parties not only reflective of ancient neofeudal social classes but further scrambled by a recent civil war that had divided much of the nation on religious lines. Shadows of the mother country's discords drifted west, where the land was by no means always bright. The first American divisions into political factions were the separatists or Republicans versus the Tories, who remained loyal to the British empire. Obviously, there were regional differences: New England's democratic town meetings versus the Virginian-Carolinian slave-owning planter aristocracy. But by and large, George Washington's 1776 diary note on his new countrymen in general and the Continental Congress in particular is not promising: "Chimney corner patriots abound: venality, corruption, prostitution of office for selfish ends, abuse of trust, perversion of funds from a national to a private use, and speculations upon the necessities of the times pervade all interests." This is pretty much what Franklin had to say of the England of 1783. But then Washington was reviewing his present, not predicting things to come.

From the beginning social differences not only between New Englanders and Virginians but within the two sections reflected the seventeenth-century division in England between Roundheads (Puritan Protestants of republican tendency) and Cavaliers (who were—or saw themselves as—landowning aristocrats, tending to monarchy). The subsequent English civil war was won by Roundheads, and the Divine Right of kings fell with King Charles's head, to be replaced by a quasi-republic with a hereditary protector, who, in turn, was superseded by the Restoration of the now-secular King Charles II. During the troubles, many edgy Cavaliers and disappointed Roundheads moved on to America, where New England got the dour Roundheads and the South got the Cavaliers or would-be Cavaliers.

John Adams brooded more than most of the founders on the intricacies of class in America. He was not in the least shy about asserting the intellectual superiority of the New English. As early as 1775: "Gentlemen, men of any sense, of any kind of education, in the other colonies are much fewer than in New England." He also noted an ominous "dissimilitude of character" in the South because "the common people among them are very ignorant and very poor. . . . This inequality of property gives an aristocratical turn to all their proceedings."

As the populist Patrick Henrys in Virginia began their complaints about the dangers of anything more than a minimal federal state, they also began their championing of states' rights, the Anti-Federalists' weapon of choice. Adams wrote Horatio Gates,

> All our misfortune arise[s] from a single source, the reluctance of the Southern colonies to republican government. The success of this war depends upon a skilful steerage of the political vessel. The difficulties lie in forming constitutions for particular colonies, and a continental constitu-

tion for the whole. . . . This can be only done on popular
principles and maxims which are so abhorrent to the incli-
nations of the barons of the South, and the proprietary interests in the middle colonies, as well as that avarice of
land which has made upon this continent so many votaries
to Mammon that I sometimes dread the consequences.

During 1775 Adams never ceased to think and analyze the
nature of what was the best government for Americans—but for
which Americans? To Mercy Otis Warren, a political activist,
Adams confided, "Monarchy is the gentlest and most fashionable
government. . . . For my own part, I am so tasteless as to prefer a
republic." Even though monarchy would supply a higher, more intricate, and voluptuous civilization, yet "under a monarchy [the
people] cannot but be vicious and foolish," while under a "well-
regulated commonwealth the people must be wise and virtuous."
But no bottle was ever half-full to an Adams. As he looked about
him at the human cards America had been dealt in this crucial year,
he found "so much rascality, so much venality and corruption, so
much avarice and ambition, such a rage for profit and commerce
among all ranks and degrees of men . . . " In far-off London,
once America was well and truly lost, *the* monarch, King George
III, found a silver thread or two in the lining of his ermine. Of his
former transatlantic subjects, he wrote, "Knavery seems to be so
much the striking feature of its inhabitants that it may not in the
end be an evil that they become aliens to this kingdom."

At home, Adams's dark broodings on his countrymen were put in a more positive light by a soon-to-be financial genius, ever eager for profits and commerce for the new nation. Alexander Hamilton, by marrying into the aristocratic Schuyler family, was the most hypergamous of the founders. Hamilton was also sternly pro-aristocratical while the Virginia "baron" Jefferson was an anti-aristocratical aristocrat. Although Washington, Adams, Jefferson, and Hamilton each favored the creation of a republic, each saw the original blueprint from a different angle. Adams alone saw virtues in monarchy—not England's, but one of our own, with titles for the men of power (due to his elliptical shape he was dubbed, His Rotundity), but Adams was too practical to try to impose on the new republic something so like what they were ridding themselves of.

Hamilton argued that every society produces a ruling class. Why not accept this given without fuss? In 1787, at Philadelphia, he opened, as it were, his closet door: "All communities divide themselves into the few and the many. The first are the rich and wellborn, then the mass of the people.... The people are turbulent and changing: they seldom judge or determine right. Give therefore to the first class a distinct permanent share in the government. They will check the unsteadiness of the second, and as they cannot receive any advantage by change, they therefore will ever maintain good government."

Adams agreed with his future political enemy, Hamilton, that the more men with a "stake in society"—property—the stronger the institutions of the state. He also approved Jefferson's granting of land to the landless, thus extending the electorate. Adams believed that "it is certain, in theory, that the only moral foundation of government is the consent of the people." Since everyone was more or less agreed upon that, the inevitable question that arose was which people. "Shall we say that every individual of the community, old and young, male and female, as well as rich and poor, must consent, expressly, to every act of legislation?" Since the founders feared majoritarian rule as much as they did royal tyranny, none of them can be accused of the slightest affection for the common man without property. But where Adams does veer from Hamilton toward Jefferson is in his adherence to Locke and Harrington and his instinctive *liberalism*, a word which is defined in our very own *Webster's Dictionary* as a tendency toward an ever-greater democracy. He puts it more sharply than Jefferson ever could in his aristocratic slave-based society. "Power," writes Adams, "always follows property. Men in general, in every society, who are wholly destitute of property, are also too little acquainted with public affairs for a right judgment, and too dependent upon other men to have a will of their own. They talk and they vote as they are directed by some man of property, who has attached their minds to his interest." With this acknowledgment, Adams becomes Jeffersonian or Jefferson Adamsian: "A balance of power on the side of equal liberty and public virtue is to make the acquisition of land easy to every member of society, to make a division of land into small quantities. . . . If the multitude is possessed of landed estates, the multitude will have the balance of power, and in that case the multitude will take care of the liberty, virtue and interest of the multitude in all acts of government."

By the time political theoreticians began to fret about the inability of socialism to put down roots in American soil, the Constitution was firmly in place to protect not only the prosperous few but, finally, the ever-enlarging "multitude"; then when the multitude eventually dwindled again to the landless few, vigorously, exploited by the prosperous fewer, new tensions developed that were only mitigated by the seemingly inexhaustible supply of land to the west and (potentially) north and south of the United States: fourscore and seven years later, President Lincoln's Homestead Act of 1862 opened up much of the western lands to settlers willing to farm some 160 acres apiece. Thus the franchise was extended to a new (if temporary) multitude, providing a golden opportunity for the corrupt, as always, to get the land away from them. But as late as 1862 the Jefferson-Adams equation was still in operation. Yet of this equation, as put forth in the 1787 Constitution, Virginia's governor, Patrick Henry, in thrall to slavery and a limited electorate, spoke for many antifederalists when he said, in his most lapidary manner, "I smell a rat."

The instinctive isolationism of political Americans has been much remarked upon (negatively by most interested parties); it has been attributed to the isolation of a republic separated by three thousand miles of ocean from wicked old Europe, the unloved source of most of our original immigrant population. Then too, the new citizens of this new republic had quite enough to do in their wild arcadia without involving themselves in the various warlike stratagems and combines of Europe. But the actual roots of our isolationism go far deeper than the protection afforded by eastern and western watery moats, as well as northern and southern borders that were usually best defended by more or less ignoring them—except on those occasions when we were trying to conquer such neighbors as Canada or Mexico.

The official discoverer of the so-called New World was the Genoese Christopher Columbus. Since he was acting in the interest of Spain, the Americas were largely a Spanish affair to begin with. But when Spain conquered such ancient wealthy kingdoms as the Aztec and Mayan and flooded Europe with American gold and silver, the financial base was established across the continent for what was to be known as the Renaissance—a rebirth of Greco-Roman civilization. By the eighteenth century, the Americas were an all-European free-for-all.

American gold paid for a lot of architecture post-1492 but it had been the fall of Constantinople to the Turks (post-1453) that sent Greek scholars with their literature and civilization west to Europe, civilizing those areas that had not enjoyed, like Spain, occupation by the Dark People or Moors. Also, decisively, the bubonic plague of the fourteenth century, after killing off much of the European population, helped spread the New World's wealth to less than multitudes. Many Europeans were inspired to emigrate to America, where their imported diseases helped decimate the native populations, with bubonic plague acting as a weapon of mass destruction. So while Europe was enjoying a rebirth of Greco-Roman culture, many of those who felt ill at ease, if not hostile, to a civilization that did not revere fundamental Christianity preferred to start over in the "new" hemisphere. As some Europeans were self-consciously trying to bring back the age of the Greek Pericles or at least that of the Roman Antonines, fundamentalist Protestants had something more dour, more pure—indeed Puritan—in view: shining cities on hills, with converted Indians and imported African slaves to do the heavy lifting.

By the time the peace treaty between England and the United States was signed in 1783, the new republic (more or less inspired by pre-Caesarian Rome) comprised the Atlantic seaboard with a large sliver of mostly English-occupied territory thrown in. The western border of the Union was the Mississippi River, controlled by the Dons, as the unloved Spanish were called.

We were now relatively free of England and her compulsive wars with France, often fought on American soil. But to the south and west there was still the ramshackle Spanish empire. Besides Texas (to become an independent republic in 1836 and an American state in 1845), Spain also controlled Florida and its western, adjacent territories. By 1819, through treaties, our busy ambassadors acquired Florida; through force, the future states of Tennessee, Mississippi, and Alabama had been unionized by 1813. That left only the potentially wealthy Spanish-Mexican "empire" to our south and west, unfurling from the Gulf of Mexico to the Pacific Ocean. Spain alone continued to be a nuisance on "our" continent. England remained a nuisance on the high seas, while Canada was a constant temptation: "our lady of the snows," as John Hay was to call her. No one doubted that one day she was bound to succumb gratefully to our arduous advances.

Otherwise, by 1800 we were relatively free of Europe except for the so-called icebox, Alaska, a property of far-off absent-minded Russia. But then history arbitrarily decided to mix in our affairs. The French Revolution of 1789 was eventually taken in hand by a young military genius called Napoleon Bonaparte, with empire on his mind.

Jefferson, when minister to France, had initially favored the revolution that ended the French monarchy whose fleet at York-town in 1781 had made possible the victory of the American Revolution. Eight years later, the French Revolution was under way. By 1793 Louis XVI and Marie Antoinette were executed and the French "continuation" of the American republican adventure depressed Adams, who doubted whether the current "French republic will last longer than the English one in the last century. I think there will be a general revolution in religion and government all over Europe." Thus he predicted, somewhat prematurely, the approaching turmoil of 1848.

Jefferson appeared tolerant of the revolutionary excesses; but he was also ignorant of their extent when he made his famous "defense" of the Revolution in which his friend, the liberal Duc de la Rochefoucauld, was murdered in the street as his wife and mother looked on. Jefferson's response to those who disapproved of revolution was stern: "The liberty of the whole world was depending on the issue of the contest, and was ever such a prize won with so little innocent blood?" Later, Jefferson would learn the true numbers of lives lost, but at the time he only saw that what he had set in motion with the Declaration of Independence had led (directly?) to the fall of an ancient despotic monarchy, and "rather than [the Revolution] should have failed I would have seen half the earth desolated. Were there but an Adam and an Eve left in every country, left free, it would be better than as it now is." This is more the raging melodrama of Marlowe's *Tamerlane* than it is Shakespeare. It is also more Rousseau than Paine, more Celtic than Anglo. In any case, no one could predict that a world conqueror was standing in the wings, ready to pick up the pieces and make an empire for himself. Adams characteristically saw no good coming from any political arrangement born of such violence.

By 1800, when Jefferson was elected president, Napoleon was dreaming of the conquest of Europe, with himself as heir if not to the emperor Augustus then to Charlemagne, an unholy Roman emperor at the very least. Napoleon's feelings toward the republic of the United States were more benign than not: after all, the

Americans could be relied on to deny France's permanent enemy, England, any part of its lost New World empire. For a moment, Napoleon, considering a transatlantic presence for himself, had forced the Spanish king to cede him all of Spain's vast territories, known as Louisiana, as well as the river-gulf port of New Orleans. But any dreams that he might have had of a base in the Western Hemisphere ended with a slave revolt in French Santo Domingo. The expense of putting down this revolt could be better applied to his plans for the conquest of Europe. Why not simply pull out of the New World?

Meanwhile, President Jefferson had instructed his minister to France, Robert R. Livingston, to offer Napoleon $10 million for New Orleans and as much property as he could get to connect with Florida to the east. The rising Virginia statesman James Monroe was also sent to Paris to negotiate the purchase of New Orleans. Like all the founders, Jefferson knew that, like it or not, the life of the new republic depended upon the volatile politics of a Europe not given to peace. Glumly, Jefferson observed that despite his own pro-French sympathies, Napoleonic France was something new and dangerous under the sun if only because the United States must now turn to England for a protective alliance against a would-be world conqueror. "The day that France takes possession of New Orleans we must marry ourselves to the British fleet and nation." In effect, the Declaration of Independence would be nullified by an admission of dependence on the hated island monarchy.

Some presidents are lucky; others not. Between the resistance of the San Dominican leader Toussaint L'Ouverture and an outbreak of yellow fever that was killing off France's best troops, Napoleon said literally, to hell with America or, in translation, "Damn sugar, damn coffee, damn colonies." Livingston was then asked how much the United States would pay for New Orleans and for *all* of Louisiana, some 828,000 square miles that could become thirteen states and all for a mere $15 million? Livingston quickly made the deal without direct instructions from Jefferson, who knew perfectly well that, great bargain or not, he could be impeached for exercising powers not granted him by the Constitution. Yet the cession of all Louisiana and New Orleans was duly signed April 30, 1803, despite Jefferson's fits of nerves and migraines. Perhaps, he suggested, a constitutional amendment should grant him permission for acquiring so many native Americans, blacks, Creoles, and irritable Spaniards as unwilling citizens. The Senate told him, in effect, to calm down while the United States, like some vast amoeba, doubled its size.

Two years later, Jefferson, reelected to a second term, sounded quite comfortable with his absorption into the Union of so many unconsulted people. In his second inaugural address, he is serenely gracious: "I know that the acquisition of Louisiana has been disapproved by some, from a candid apprehension that the enlargement of our territory could endanger its union. But who can limit the extent to which the federative principle may operate effectively? . . . And in any view, is it not better that the opposite bank of the Mississippi should be settled by our own brethren and children, than by strangers of another family?"

Finally, the ambassadors concluded their task of keeping Europe not only out of American affairs but, indeed, out of the entire Western Hemisphere. In 1846 President Polk observed: "We must have California." Since that Pacific littoral was part of Mexico, Polk provoked Mexico into a war with the United States. California, Arizona, and Utah were ceded two years later. More peacefully, the tidy-minded Polk acquired the Pacific Northwest by treaties with England. With the acquisition of Oregon, Washington, and Idaho, the Union now filled the continent from sea to shining sea. In 1867 the Russians sold us their icebox, Alaska, while Hawaii was annexed in 1898, along with Puerto Rico and the reluctant Philippines. While this filling in of vast spaces with neatly ruled new states, Secretary of State John Quincy Adams produced for President James Monroe a doctrine declaring that the two American continents were off limits to Europe, as Europe would be to us. In 1917, by entering World War I, we in effect voided the Monroe Doctrine. But that was to gain yet another world, one that is currently—optimistically—called "global."

Benjamin Franklin proved to be our most effective ambassador. He was not only a successful businessman-publisher-writer and general wise man, he was also an early proponent of paper currency (to keep his printing presses busy, some said). Although he appeared to be the essence of solid bourgeois common sense and propriety, he had a son out of wedlock who later became, as royal governor of New Jersey, an active opponent of the Revolution. The not-so-easygoing Franklin never forgave him. Later, Franklin had a common-law union with a woman who bore him a son and a daughter. Later, in Europe, to the consternation of his fellow American ambassadors, he had joyous affairs with great ladies as well as humble ones. He even produced some notes for young men on the advantages of taking an older woman for mistress.

Adams was the reverse of Dr. Franklin in everything except intelligence. Adams thought Franklin lazy when he was simply diplomatic or cautious and a hypocrite when he was simply charming. Franklin's great popularity—and self-promotion—so distressed Adams that with Franklin in mind he wrote a friend, "A man must be his own trumpeter, he must write or dictate paragraphs of praise in the newspapers, he must dress, have a retinue and equipage, he must ostentatiously publish to the world his own writings with his name, write even panegyrics on them, he must get his picture drawn, his statue made, and must hire all the artists in his turn, to set about works to spread his name, make the mob stare and gape and perpetuate his fame." Adams could not believe that Franklin's popularity with court and intellectuals and the French in general might be due to a nature opposite to his own. Of Franklin, inventor of the astonishing eponymous stove and experimenter in electricity, Adams could only remark sourly that because of his popularity in high circles he was "in a constant state of dissipation." Nevertheless, French admiration for Franklin extended even to the secret police, who noted that during one of their homeland secret searches of his belongings, his underwear was the whitest they had ever seen.

In 1784 Thomas Jefferson was appointed minister to France, joining Franklin and Adams. He served until 1789. It is a triple irony that three of the principal inventors of the United States should have been abroad in Europe during the Constitution-making period that was presided over by Washington and largely created by James Madison and Alexander Hamilton. But the ambassadors were doing necessary work not only in matters of trade and public relations but in the intricate business of borrowing money for the embryo republic, much of it from Dutch bankers who particularly esteemed Adams.

The widower Jefferson delighted both Adamses, and the censorious Abigail plainly had no knowledge of Sally Hemings, the young mulatto slave in Jefferson's household (who arrived, in any case, later), but she must have known something of his passion for a married woman, Maria Cosway. Jefferson, plainly in a state of euphoria, wrote Abigail a letter reflective of his renewed joy in life at Paris, "where we have singing, dancing, laughter and merriment. . . . When our king goes out, they fall down and kiss the earth. . . . Then they go to kissing one another. This is the truest wisdom. They have as much happiness in one year as one Englishman in ten." Shrewd Abigail must have got the range. Maria's husband, Richard, painted miniatures, unaware that his rival was painting, in quite another dimension, a huge fresco of empire aborning.

The Adamses returned to Paris from London to greet Jefferson, who, together with Franklin, John Jay, and Henry Laurens, was a part of the American commission to negotiate a final peace with England. Jefferson's "immoral" life might have disturbed John and Abigail, but his amiability and broad culture so entranced the New England couple that gossip simply did not adhere to him as it did to Dr. Franklin, who managed to shock Abigail when she was greeted by his ancient ladyfriend Madame Helvétius. At table, Madame Helvétius sat between Franklin and Adams and talked incessantly. Her lapdog received as many kisses as Franklin himself. When the little dog squatted beside the table, Madame serenely cleaned up the mess with her chemise. Abigail was torn between disgust and absolute joy, giving rise to an Adamsian sermon to a friend apropos Franklin's being so much embraced by this lady, "He cannot be averse to the example of King David, for if embraces will tend to prolong his life and promote the vigor of his circulation, he is in a fair way to live the age of an antediluvian." Jefferson must have seen in Franklin a soul somewhat similar to his own. When the gout-ridden Franklin finally left Paris on July 12, 1785, in the Queen's litter, drawn by placid Spanish mules, Jefferson replaced him as minister to France. Except, as Jefferson said at the time, "No one can replace him. . . . I am only his successor. . . . Benjamin Franklin was the greatest man and ornament of the age and country in which he lived." Adams held his peace. Franklin's verdict on Adams was Olympian: "He means well for his country, is always an honest man, often a wise one, but sometimes and in some things absolutely out of his senses."

Jefferson was more generous to the soon-to-be vice president of the United States. After working with Adams, he noted what Adams had himself also noted: "A degree of vanity . . . too attentive to ceremony . . . irritable and a bad calculator of the forces and probable effect of the motives which govern men"; that, Jefferson told Madison, "is all the ill which can possibly be said of him." It was quite enough. No man who is a bad calculator of those forces which govern men ought to be president, as time would demonstrate.

Four

April 12, 1789: a Mr. Sylvester Bourne arrived in Braintree, Massachusetts. He had come from the First U.S. Congress to notify Mr. John Adams that he had been elected vice president. The actual vote was not directly cast by those few men qualified to vote for various state officers as well as the House of Representatives but by their long shadow, the Electoral College, which consisted of those who had themselves been elected and so made up what Hamilton hoped would be, if not the very best people, at least the most propertied and esteemed locally.

After the ratification of the Constitution, the last Continental Congress made way for a national Congress of the States, optimistically known as *United*. The Congress set January 7, 1789, as the day for the selection of the Electoral College, February 4

for their election of the president, and March 4 for the inauguration of the first administration of the republic. Each state
had its own method of selecting presidential electors as well
as members of the Congress. After choosing New York City
as the temporary capital (always temporary as long as Philadelphia lusted for the honor), the Continental Congress gave up
the ghost.

Adams had known for some weeks of his election; and he was
already packed for his journey. But, as was usual for him, this
apparently golden apple contained a bitter worm secretly introduced by Secretary of the Treasury–to–be Alexander Hamilton,
the unofficial leader of the national Federalist Party, much as
James Madison led the Republicans. Political parties as such did
not yet exist, but since foreign affairs dominated the life of the
new republic, the great division was between those who still adhered to things British—the Federalists—and "the French party":
the Republicans who looked to Thomas Jefferson as their icon
for all seasons. Jefferson not only was pro-French but while American minister to France had actually taken secret part in the early
days of the Revolution.

When it came to the mechanics of presidential elections, the
Constitution had rather light-heartedly ruled that the candidate
who got the most votes in the Electoral College would become
president, while the runner-up would become the vice president.
This deliberately ignored the matter of faction or party, which
came to a head in 1796, when the Proto-Federalist Adams was

elected president while the Proto-Republican Jefferson became vice president. In 1804 the Twelfth Amendment allowed for party interest by requiring separate balloting for president and vice president. The Electoral College, however, remains to this day solidly in place to ensure that majoritarian governance can never interfere with those rights of property that the founders believed not only inalienable but possibly divine.

At first, Adams was unaware that Hamilton meant to control the new government. Washington was aging, and Hamilton still knew how to play surrogate son. Washington himself was a highly competent, even awesome, chief executive. But though he could run the War Department unassisted, the treasury was beyond his capacities: Hamilton was given a free hand because, within the Federalist faction, only Adams was of equal intelligence, learning, and experience: in Adams's ambassadorial years abroad, raising money for the Revolution, he was known and trusted by Europe's principal bankers, particularly those in the Netherlands. Sidelined to the vice presidency, he was hardly a threat to Hamilton. But Hamilton enjoyed unscrupulous detail work for its own sake. He saw to it that Adams would get a minimal vote in no way commensurate with his standing in the nation. Where Washington got the College's entire sixty-nine votes, Adams got only thirty-four, while ten candidates divided the remaining thirty-five. Adams was a humiliating poor second which should minimize his influence.

Furiously, Adams wrote a friend that he was tempted to reject the election. "Is not my election to this office, in the scurvy manner in which it was done, a curse rather than a blessing? Is this justice? Is there no common sense or decency in the business? Is it an indelible stain on our country, countrymen, and constitution? I assure you I think so." Unaware of the busy Hamilton, Adams feared that he and his true-blue Federalists had paled to nothing in the great light that George Washington shed all around him. Was not he, John Adams, if nothing else, New England incarnate?

Adams was, of course, in place, presiding over the Senate on April 30 when President Washington took the oath of office. All the principal founders were on hand except for Jefferson, who was in France. Washington had offered him the secretaryship for foreign affairs (which promptly elided into domestic affairs as well under the bleak, overall title of secretary of "state"), General Knox was war, John Jay was chief justice of the United States, Edmund Randolph was attorney general, unencumbered by a Department of Justice.

The new vice president's first day on the job did not augur well for what would prove to be eight years of presiding over the Senate, which met on the second floor of Federal Hall. (The House of Representatives was on the first floor.)

Adams delivered a two-page speech: "Unaccustomed to refuse any public service, however dangerous to my reputation or disproportionate to my talents, it would have been inconsistent to have adopted another maxim of conduct at this time." Plainly, the indelible stain of those too few votes had not entirely faded as he stood now in history's etiolating glare. "When the prosperity of the country and the liberties of the people require perhaps as much as ever the attention of those who possess any share of the public confidence." Then Adams gazed upon the two dozen new senators and really laid it on, calling them "celebrated defenders of the liberties of this country, whom menaces could not intimidate, corruption seduce, nor flattery allure; those intrepid asserters of the rights of mankind whose philosophy and policy have enlightened the world in twenty years more than it was ever enlightened in many centuries by ancient scholars or modern universities." The senators calmly accepted this praise—Was it not simply their due? The American megalomaniacal style of self-praise was now in place. Only Pennsylvania's William Maclay, a fairly constant critic of Adams, found his rhetoric "heavy."

Once Adams appeared firmly in charge of himself and the Senate, he proceeded to fall apart. First, he was confused about protocol. Was the president to be called His Excellency or, better, his Mightiness? Adams asked the Senate (intrepid asserters of the "rights of man") how he ought to behave when the President entered the chamber to take the oath of office. "I feel great difficulty, how to act. I am possessed of two separate powers—the one in *esse*, the other in *posse*. . . . When the president comes into the Senate, what shall I *be*? I wish, gentlemen, to think what shall I be?" Confused, as it turned out. Adams spoke of the value of titles. Republicans disagreed. The discussion continued until

General Washington appeared in the chamber. He wore a dark brown suit with silver buttons, white stockings, black shoes with square silver buckles, and a sword. Adams escorted him to the presidential chair. Washington sat. Adams stood and tried to recall the brief speech of welcome that he had prepared, but he had forgotten every word. Finally, desperately, he indicated that Washington should accompany him to the balcony of the chamber. A large crowd had gathered in the street below that was— and is—called Wall. Then New York's Chancellor Robert R. Livingston administered the oath of office. The crowd gave three cheers for the president, who bowed to them: then he and Adams withdrew into the chamber where the president delivered his inaugural address. Senators noted that his hands were shaking from tension. As he now faced the triumphant completion of his life's work, he seemed somber, and his voice trembled as he read what was not so much a declaration of the commencement of a reign as a farewell to himself who had brought them all to this place and time. Many senators wept, overwhelmed by pity for the aging man, and awe at what he had done. John Adams also wept.

It has not been recorded whether Adams wept when he was told that Congress had not only not voted a salary for the vice president but had made no financial allowance of any kind for him. He told Abigail not to come to New York until Congress took up its first—and never-ending—task, the raising of revenues to support the new government. In the House of Representatives, Madison proposed a series of tariffs in order to finance the new government. As luck would have it, the first tax proposed was six cents on molasses, New England's principal import. The "neutral" president of the Senate promptly went to work for his fellow New Englanders; together they got the tax down to four cents, which was approved—but not before Adams had suggested three cents instead of four. After molasses came loafsugar, a major war in which Maclay of sugar loaf–producing Pennsylvania was a general. There was a tie vote and the vice president broke the tie in favor of the tax, earning more bad reviews from Maclay. Then came salt . . . The days of discussing Hume and Montesquieu were over.

Maclay noted that, periodically, during debate, Adams would start wriggling in his chair until, finally, "up he got to tell us all about how he had, with Mr. Jefferson, appointed Mr. Barclay to the Emperor of Morocco . . . " Adams was Adams, to the end, a born schoolmaster.

Eventually, the vice president was salaried and joined by Abigail. The Adamses were then able to move into a Hudson River mansion called Richmond Hill, destined one day to be the paradisal estate of Aaron Burr, first as Alexander Hamilton's rival at the New York bar and then, when political parties began to cohere, as his rival for the mastery of New York State. In that showdown Burr was the Republican ally of populist Tammany Hall, while Federalist Hamilton was even more highly placed as secretary of the treasury—in effect, Washington's prime minister. As the Anglophile Hamilton happily noted, the English prime minister's primacy was based on his occupying the similar office of first lord of the treasury.

Since the tradition had not yet been established that the wives of presidents and vice presidents are doomed to be at odds, Abigail and Lady Washington, as Martha was generally and voluntarily known, got on splendidly. Abigail found Martha a bit plump but confessed that, even so, she had a much better figure than Abigail.

At the Washington's first dinner party for the Adamses, Abigail was amused to call the president (for whom Adams—uninvited?—had made such a fuss about titling) Your Majesty. The sharp-tongued Abigail was all honey in describing Washington: "a singular example of modesty and diffidence" whose dignity, even majesty, far surpassed that of his rival over the water, King George III, who had made a disagreeable impression on her.

At dinner, the Washingtons faced each other at the center of a long table with a flowery centerpiece. Since neither president nor vice president had much in the way of conversation, the huge dinner, served by liveried footmen and waiters, was consumed in relative silence. Senator Maclay was on hand to mock so much pseudoroyal ceremony. We are told that the dinner began with soup (what kind?); next came various fish boiled and roasted, then roast game, geese, duck (presumably canvasback, which was so popular that the breed was extinct by the end of the next century, along with the southern turtle known as terrapin); finally, they were served apple pies, puddings, ice cream, jellies, fruits, nuts. When the table was in some haste cleared, the president drank the health of each guest in rapid succession until Maclay was worried that he would be "thrown out in the hurry, but I got a little wine in my glass and passed the ceremony."

The dinner reminded John Adams that although his salary—finally set—was one-fourth that of the president, he was obliged to entertain just as lavishly, with the entire Senate as his ever-hungry extended family. He complained to his son John Quincy that his remuneration was a sort of "curiosity." One reason for these hurried silent dinners were the principals' absence of teeth for the task. Washington had two wooden plates containing ivory teeth that Madeira wine tended to stain, while Adams was losing tooth after tooth but refused to install hinged plates for fear of looking as grim as Washington now did. He ate with difficulty; and spoke with the pronounced lisp of the dentally challenged, to use a twenty-first-century locution.

Once the table was cleared, Lady Washington led the ladies upstairs to a drawing room, and the men passed the port round the table and listened as President Washington told a complicated "funny" story about a clergyman who lost his hat and wig while crossing the Brunks River. (To this day professional comedians maintain that, to get a laugh, there must be a *k* in a key word.) At story's end, Washington smiled to celebrate the story's end and the gentlemen laughed uproariously; then the president herded them upstairs to join the ladies.

***

Adams eventually came to enjoy his situation as arbiter of the Senate. He also immersed himself in the classics, studying earlier attempts at government on republican lines. He noted that political groupings were beginning to form along what might prove to be fault lines in the new Constitution. The two principal groupings—the British party and the French party—further were split by the executive party's jealousy over what it perceived as the Senate's usurpation of presidential power. This division also represented the nation's geographical division, represented by the Mason-Dixon line, to whose north were the Middle States and New England and to whose south were what would one day become the secessionist slave-holding states of the ill-fated Confederacy.

Washington and Secretary of War Knox visited the Senate with a bundle of treaties involving various Indian tribes. The president, conforming to the Constitution in the matter of treaty making, wished to gain the "advice and consent" of the Senate. Adams surrendered his chair to Washington. Knox then presented Washington with a stack of documents which Washington then gave his vice president to read to the Senate. In turn,

Adams gave the documents to the Secretary of the Senate, aware that his toothless lisp would be made no clearer to his auditors by a jam of carriages below the chamber in Wall Street. Next there were seven questions about the treaty on which Washington wanted the Senate's advice and consent. Adams had started on the first question when a senator asked him to read the treaty through again. Adams reread the treaty as well as the first question and then asked, by rote, "Do you advise and consent?" There was an edgy silence which Adams mistook for agreement. But before he could continue with the other questions, the ever-reliable Maclay rose to say that this was no way to conduct such a complicated and delicate business. The executive should submit all relevant documents to the Senate, where a special committee would study them with the attention they deserved. Implicit in this rebuke was an insistence on the legislative branch's coequality with the executive, made all the more intolerable by the presence of the first magistrate himself in the chair of the presiding officer of the Senate.

Washington, in a fury, said, "This defeats every purpose of my coming here." He had come in good faith with the secretary of war to describe in detail the treaties and answer the questions. Now the whole process would be subject to delay. But if that was their choice . . . Washington rose from his chair, bowed and withdrew. He had, Maclay happily noted, "a discontented air."

The first battle between the court party, as the upholders

of the executive were called, and those—like Adams—eager to curb the "aristocratic" Senate was won by the Senate. An on-going war with victory sometimes for the one, sometimes for the other until 1941, when Congress declared war for the last time, thus allowing its greatest constitutional power to go, by default, to the executive.

In November 1789, after an absence of five years, Thomas Jefferson was back in Virginia for a short stay: he expected to return to Paris in the spring and resume his embassy. But on December 11 he received a letter from Washington appointing him secretary of state. Jefferson was of two minds. He very much wanted to observe the course of the French Revolution firsthand, acting as a secret adviser to the Marquis de Lafayette. He also did not want to be in charge of fisheries or whatever other humble domestic departments might be huddled beneath the State Department's roof. But Madison thought it politically necessary that Jefferson be at the head of the cabinet, while Washington himself conde-scended to plead: "So far as I have been able to obtain informa-tion from all quarters, your late appointment has given very ex-tensive and very great satisfaction to the Public."

On February 14 Jefferson accepted the post. On February 23, 1790, Jefferson's daughter Martha was married at Monticello to a third cousin, Thomas Mann Randolph Jr. Presumably, on the scene was her youthful aunt the slave Sally Hemings, daughter of Martha's grandfather, John Wayles. The fact that Jefferson would have six children by Sally (half-sister to his beloved wife, another Martha) has been a source of despair to many old-guard historians, but, unhappily for them, recent DNA testings establish consanguinity between the Hemingses and their master, whose ambivalences about slavery (not venery) are still of central concern to us. If all men are created equal, then, if you are serious, free your slaves, Mr. Jefferson. But they were his capital. He could not and survive, and so he did not. He even transferred six families of slaves to daughter Martha and her husband. It might be useful for some of his overly correct critics to try to put themselves in his place. But neither empathy nor compassion is an American trait. Witness, the centuries of black slavery taken for granted by much of the country.

Unable to find a house on Broadway, Jefferson found one at 57 Maiden Lane. Jefferson's State Department was manned by two chief clerks, two assistant clerks, and a translator. Budget for the office staff, including his own salary ($3,500 per annum), was $8,000. Since France was the republic's most powerful ally, he insisted on a minister plenipotentiary for that nation. Washington agreed but said that should England send us a minister, we would send them one. Otherwise, lower-level diplomats were used. Chargés d'affaires to Madrid and Lisbon, a consul to Morocco to keep an eye on the shores of Tripoli, whose pirates were harassing our shipping.

Senator Maclay was sour, begrudging every penny spent on foreign missions: "I know not a single thing that we have for a minister to do in a single court in Europe. . . . Indeed, the less we have to do with them the better." A few years later Jefferson would have the last laugh when his envoys to France got us Louisiana.

But Maclay's contribution to history was not statecraft; rather, it was his pen. He is our rustic Saint Simon. Montaigne used to complain about writers of history who never told you what any-one looked like (particularly on the deathbed). But this is how Jefferson looked to Maclay on May 24, 1790. Jefferson was being questioned by a Senate committee. Maclay's diary:

> When I came to the Hall Jefferson and the rest of the
> committee were there. Jefferson is a slender man. Has
> rather the air of Stiffness in his manner. His clothes seem
> too small for him. He sits in a lounging Manner on one
> hip, and with one of his shoulders elevated much above
> the other. His face has a scrany Aspect. His whole figure
> has a loose schackling Air. He had a rambling Vacant
> look and nothing of that firm collected deportment which
> I expected would dignify the presence of a secretary or
> Minister. I looked for Gravity, but a laxity of Manner,
> seemed shed about him. He spoke almost without ceasing.

But even his discourse partook of his personal demeanor. It was loose and rambling and yet he scattered information wherever he went, and some even brilliant Sentiments sparkled from him.

We now know he was suffering from migraine. Later in life visitors found him charming but somewhat rigid in his opinions; he did not like contradiction. Maclay makes him sound like a peripatetic philosopher, but in the end he was, as he began, an unswerving believer that this world was for the living and that he, for one, had enlisted in "the holy cause of freedom." He seemed oddly unaware of the inconsistencies in his nature. Fortunately, he was stabilized throughout his life by James Madison, now serving as the leader of the "Republican" faction in the House of Representatives. Where Jefferson had a wild attachment, at times, to radical sentiments, Madison could usually calm him down.

Meanwhile, the secretary of the treasury, having sidetracked his rival economist to the vice presidency, had now, with Washington's bemused blessing, taken over the finances of the republic. In January 1790 Hamilton submitted his report on the public credit to Congress. He wanted Congress not only to fund the national debt but to assume all debts incurred by the individual states during the Revolution. Since Hamilton was also making himself busy in Jefferson's foreign affairs, Jefferson returned the compliment and joined with Madison in the all-important matter of the nation's finances. The states' indebtedness was the first battleground. Congress split on the issue of federal assumption of their debts.

That corruption of the citizenry which Franklin acknowledged, and in the long run feared, had now reared its head. Hamilton's plan to pay off the domestic debt at par set off an alarm bell for Madison. Speculators had been busy buying up depreciated securities from humble investors, anticipating huge profits once Hamilton redeemed all this paper at par. Madison went into action. He proposed to Congress that only original buyers of the securities be paid at par value with arrears of interest, while later speculators should be denied their potentially spectacular profits, having purchased for pennies the apparently worthless bonds of the Continental Congress. Congress, which knew a thing or two about making money out of "insider trading," rejected Madison's amendment. Also, Congress was now divided between willing states with large debts and those—unwilling—with small. Jefferson feared that on this great financial issue the Union might split and "burst, and vanish and the states separate to take care everyone of itself." What to do? How effect a compromise?

Over the years Jefferson tended to give different versions of events in his life. He was perfectly human in his desire to appear always in the right, not to mention the tricks that time does to memory. (In old age he said he read only one newspaper and promptly forgot what he had just read.) Finally, there was the havoc that later information could have upon what he curiously called "false facts," suggesting that the untrue fact also has some sort of Platonic essentiality. Yet he did his best not to be too much at odds with his own earlier version of events. The relationship with Hamilton is a case in point. Jefferson did not like the way that Hamilton used his closeness to Washington to influence—even alter—the policies of the secretary of state. Hamilton's Anglophilia he took for granted, much as he did Adams's affection for English political institutions. They, in turn, when not in crisis, were tolerant of his Frenchness, but as the first administration of President Washington began to turn stormy in the battle over the federal assumption of the states' debts, relations between the three were edgy.

In old age Jefferson assembled what has been called *The Anas 1791–1806*. He was ready now to set the record straight by placing his bust (by Houdon) in a favorable light. He begins amiably:

> In these three vols. will be found copies of the official
> opinions given in writing by me to Genl. Washington,
> while I was Secretary of State, with sometimes the docu-
> ments belonging to the case. . . . Some of these are the
> rough draughts, some press-copies, some fair ones. In the
> earlier part of my acting in that office I took no other note
> of the passing transactions: but, after a while, I saw the

importance of doing it, in aid of my memory. Very often therefore I made memorandums on loose scraps of paper, taken out of my pocket in the moment and laid by to be copied fair at leisure, which however they hardly ever were.

This rings absolutely true, proving that sloth often alters truth more than mere mendacity.

These scraps therefore, ragged, rubbed, & scribbled as they were, I had bound with the others by a binder who came into my cabinet, did it under my own eye, and without the opportunity of reading a single paper. At this day [February 4, 1818], at the lapse of 25 years, or more, from their dates, I have given to the whole a calm revisal, when the passions of the time are passed away, and the reasons of the transactions act alone on the judgment. Some of the information I had recorded are now cut out from the rest, because I have seen that they were incorrect, or doubtful, or merely personal or private, with which we have nothing to do.

Thus, a sovereign himself writes court history. But this sovereign has a canny working relationship with history. Jefferson's second thoughts are usually more interesting than his first, with which he often prefers to have nothing to do later. He anticipates skeptical witnesses:

I should perhaps have thought the rest not worth preserving, but for their testimony against the only history of that

period which pretends to have been compiled from authentic and unpublished documents. Could these documents, all, be laid open to the public eye, they might be
compared, contrasted, weighed and the truth fairly lifted
out of them, for we are not to suppose that everything
found among Genl. Washington's papers is to be taken as
gospel truth. . . . With him were deposited suspicions &
certainties, rumors and realities, facts and falsehoods. . . .
From such a Congeries history may be made to wear any
hue, with which the passions of the compiler, royalist or
republican, may cause to tinge it.

Jefferson's grudges were deep-rooted. He particularly de-
tested the author of "the only history of that period which pretends to have been compiled from authentic and unpublished
documents." So who was this false historian? None other than
the chief justice of the United States, John Marshall, his cousin
and lifelong Tory foe. Marshall's *Life of Washington* was hurried
into the world to demonstrate how like subject and biographer
were in so many great matters. Jefferson now must overthrow, if
not Marshall's thus far unsuspected masterpiece of guile *Marbury
v. Madison*, at least the Supreme Court's right to review on constitutional grounds the laws of Congress and decrees of presidents and, in the process, regain Washington for the Republican
cause. This is first-rate destructive criticism which succeeds in
placing Washington at the center of the republic he had set in

motion: "Let no man believe that Genl. Washington ever intended that his papers should be used for the suicide of the cause, for which he had lived . . . "

To demonstrate that Washington was no royalist or aristocrat, Jefferson notes his own objections to the Society of the Cincinnati, a would-be hereditary order of military officers. Jefferson maintains that some of the officers who created the Cincinnati had also proposed, before the army disbanded, that Washington become king with their support. "The indignation with which he is said to have scouted this parricide proposition, was equally worthy of his virtue and wisdom." Close readers of Jefferson can now tell that, soon, he will drop the name of Colonel Hamilton. He does. He mentions Hamilton's proposal at the Constitutional Convention to adopt a government that combined royalism and republicanism. Executive and one of the other branches were to be appointed for life (those Polish kings again). When this was rejected, Hamilton left, "desperate." Jefferson makes his case firmly. But he relies a good deal on memory long after the fact. He seems not to have known that Washington nearly gave up the presidency of the Constitutional Convention on account of a prior engagement with the Society of the Cincinnati. Jefferson tells us that Washington had assured him that he himself was "fully determined to use all his endeavors for its total suppression." Thus the father of his country gave out half loaves to his troublesome sons.

The *Anas* are very much Jefferson's "my side of the matter," often recollected in a suspiciously fierce storm of apparent tranquillity. He tells us of his arrival in the new capital as secretary of state.

> The President received me cordially. . . . The courtesies of dinner parties given me as a stranger newly arrived among them, placed me at once in their familiar society. But I cannot describe the wonder and mortification with which the table conversations filled me. Politics were the chief topic, and a preference of kingly, over republican, government, was evidently the favorite. An apostate I could not be; nor yet a hypocrite: and I found myself, for the most part, the only advocate on the republican side . . .

Thus, he clears his throat, as it were, to take up the vexing subject of the monarchical Hamilton.

> Hamilton's financial system had then past. It had two objects. 1st as a puzzle, to exclude popular understanding and inquiry. 2dly, as a machine for the corruption of the legislature; for he avowed the opinion that man could be governed by one of two motives only, force or interest: force, he observed, in this country was out of the question; and the interests therefore of the members must be laid hold of, to keep the legislature in union with the Executive.

And with grief and shame it must be admitted that his machine was not without effect. That even in this, the birth of our government, some members were found sordid enough to bend their duty to their interests, and to look after personal, rather than public good.

It is a disconcerting characteristic of the Jeffersonian high moral style that he falls so easily into practiced cadences that suggest nothing so much as the higher hypocrisy. By 1790 he had been a Virginia legislator, a Virginia governor, as well as a member of national congresses. He knew perfectly well what the wheeling and dealing of opposing forces eventually comes down to: all right, I'll reduce the tax on your salt by two cents if you grant me the placement of a navy yard at Norfolk here in Virginia. The complexities of what it has amused us to refer to as pork barrel politics is the essence of governance by unlovely compromise. New England gives up X in exchange for Pennsylvania's Y. Was it not ever thus in a republic? But there was something in Hamilton's bald, bright acceptance of interest as the universal key that set Jefferson's teeth on edge. For one thing, Hamilton and aides had left themselves open to the charge of corruption in the matter of those citizens who had been obliged to sell their certificates of debt to speculators. "Hamilton made no difference between the original holders, & the fraudulent purchasers of this paper." When Congress voted redemption at par, those in the know were quick to send couriers all over the Union to buy from the unwitting what was thought to be worthless paper. "Immense sums were thus filched from the poor & Ignorant, and fortunes accumulated by those who had themselves been poor enough before." Jefferson strikes an even more somber note: "Men thus enriched by the dexterity of a leader, would follow of course the chief who was leading them to fortune, and become the zealous instruments of all his enterprises." So in addition to the royally and republican inclined factions there was now a Hamiltonian bandit party of new-rich, thanks to his masterful manipulations at the treasury. Happily,

this game was over, and another was on the carpet at the moment of my arrival; and to this I was most ignorantly & innocently made to hold the candle. This fiscal maneuver is well known by the name of the Assumption. Independently of the debts of Congress, the states had, during the war, contracted separate and heavy debts; and Massachusetts particularly in an absurd attempt, absurdly conducted on the British post of Penobscot: and the more debt Hamilton could rake up, the more plunder for his mercenaries. This money, whether wisely or foolishly spent, was pretended to have been spent for general purposes, and ought therefore to be paid from the general purse. But it was objected that nobody knew what these debts were, what their amount, or what their proofs. No matter; we will guess them to be 20. millions. But of these 20. millions

we do not know how much should be reimbursed to one
state, nor how much to another. No matter; we will guess.
And so another scramble was set on foot among the several
states, and some got much, some little, some nothing. But
the main object was sustained: the phalanx of the Treasury
was reinforced by additional recruits. This measure produced the most bitter and angry contest ever known in
Congress before or since the union of the states. I arrived
in the midst of it . . . but a stranger to the ground . . . I took
no concern in it.

Thus he steps to one side, as yet unaware that corruption now
has a powerful faction led by the amoral Hamilton.

Nevertheless, Hamilton's measure narrowly lost in the House
of Representatives. "Hamilton was in despair. As I was going to
the President's one day, I met him in the street. He walked me
backwards & forwards before the President's door for half an
hour. He painted pathetically the temper into which the legislature had been wrought, the disgust of those who were called the
Creditor states, the danger of the secession of their members,
and the separation of the states." Hamilton begged Jefferson to
rally enough of his friends around him in order to allow the Assumption legislation to pass, showing that a united cabinet had
rallied round the president who was central to this—and every—
matter. "I told him that I was really a stranger to the whole subject; not having yet informed myself of the system of finances

adopted," and so, he tells us, he separates himself from the business, pleading ignorance. But "I proposed to him however to dine with me the next day, and I would invite another friend or two, bringing them into conference together, and I thought it impossible that reasonable men, consulting together coolly, could fail, by some mutual sacrifices of opinion to form a compromise which was to save the union." The discussion took place (Jefferson names no names, but Madison was there). "I could take no part in it." It was agreed certain votes would be changed and the vote of rejection of Hamilton's measure would be rescinded. Jefferson, the philosopher king, now mildly notes: "It was observed that the bill would be peculiarly bitter to the Southern states, and that some concomitant measure should be adopted to sweeten it a little to them. There had before been propositions to fix the seat of government either at Philadelphia or at Georgetown on the Potomac; and it was thought by giving it to Philadelphia for ten years, and to Georgetown permanently afterwards, this might, as an anodyne, calm in some degree the ferment which might be excited by the other measure alone."

And so the Assumption was past, and a 20. millions of stock divided among favored states, and thrown in as pabulum to the stock-jobbing herd. This added to the number of votaries to the treasury and made its Chief the master of every vote in the legislature which might give to the government the direction suited to his political views. I know well and so must be understood, that nothing like a majority in Congress had yielded to this corruption. Far from it. But a division, not very unequal, had already taken place in the honest part of that body, between the parties styled republican and federal. The latter being monarchists in principle, adhered to Hamilton of course, as their leader in that principle, and this mercenary phalanx added to them ensured him always a majority in both houses: so the whole action of the legislature was now under the direction of the treasury.

Jefferson's part in the creation of the Hamiltonian political and fiscal system he puts down to his own ignorance and innocence of what was going on at the time. In retrospect, he realizes that in a nation without, as yet, political parties as opposed to factions, Hamilton was successfully transforming his sort of Federalists into a majority party with absolute control, through the higher corruption, in Jefferson's eyes, of the legislature. This makes it all the more interesting that the triumph of Hamilton's usurpation of power, the creation of the Bank of the United States, the *Anas* passes over in an aside. Jefferson does note that the members of Congress who gave Hamilton his majorities for the Assumption and the funding system would, in the normal course leave office and in their place "some engine of influence more permanent must be contrived. This engine was the Bank of the US. All that history is known; so I shall say nothing about it." He did, of course, say more in his memo to President Washington (February 15, 1791), *On the Constitutionality of a National Bank.* Since the Constitution did not allow for such a bank, Jefferson said it was a matter for the States. Hamilton argued that where the Constitution was silent the Federal government could act.

Jefferson is quick to argue that in this matter, contrary to rumor, his party was in no way opposed to General Washington, Hamilton's protector,

> for he was not aware of the drift or of the effect of Hamilton's schemes. Unversed in financial projects & calculations, & budgets, his approbation of them was bottomed on his confidence in the man. But Hamilton was not only a monarchist, but for a monarchy bottomed on corruption. In proof of this I will relate an anecdote, for the truth of which I attest the God who made me. Before the President set out on his Southern tour in April 1791, he addressed a letter of the 4th of that month, from Mount Vernon to the Secretaries of State, Treasury and War, desiring that if any serious and important cases should arise during his absence, they could consult and act on them, and he requested that the Vice-president should also be consulted. This was the only occasion on which that officer was ever requested to take part in a Cabinet question [a mild dig at Adams's peripheral role].

An occasion arose when Jefferson assembled the Cabinet and vice president to discuss some matter. After they had dined,

conversation began on other matters and, by some circumstance was led to the British constitution, on which Mr. Adams observed, "Purge that constitution of its corruption and give to its popular branch equality of representation, and it would be the most perfect constitution ever devised by the wit of man." Hamilton paused and said, "purge it of its corruption and give to its popular branch equality of presentation, & it would become an impracticable government: as it stands at present, with all its supposed defects, it is the most perfect government which ever existed." And this was assuredly the exact line which separated the political creeds of these two gentlemen. The one was for two hereditary branches and an honest elective one: the other for a hereditary king with a house of lords and commons, corrupted to his will, and standing between him and the people.

Hamilton was indeed a singular character. Of acute understanding, disinterested, honest and honorable in all private transactions, amiable in society, and honorable in all and duly valuing virtue in private life, yet so bewitched & perverted by the British example, as to be under thoro' conviction that corruption was essential to the government of a nation.

Mr. Adams had originally been a republican. The glare of royalty and nobility, during his mission to England, had made him believe their fascination a necessary ingredient in government, and Shays's rebellion, not sufficiently understood where he then was, seemed to prove that the absence of want and oppression was not a sufficient guarantee of order. His book on the American constitution having made known his political biases, he was taken up by the monarchical federalists in his absence, and on his return to the U.S., he was by them made to believe that the general disposition of our citizens was favorable to monarchy. . . . Mr. Adams, I am sure, has been long since convinced of the treacheries with which he was surrounded during his administration.

It is not often that a principal character in history throws so much light on his rivals that, in the process, he himself is illuminated; shadowed, too. It is difficult, for instance, to believe that Jefferson was not aware of every detail of the famous bargain with Hamilton which gave Hamilton his majorities in House and Senate and gave the Virginians the capital of the country not far from Mount Vernon, whose proprietor bought two lots in what would become the world's least likely seat of government.

In Congress and cabinet and, perhaps, in the CEO heart of George Washington, the Hamilton system flourished. The Bank, located in Philadelphia, was an instant success. Years later Daniel Webster eulogized Hamilton in gorgeous metaphors. "He smote the rock of the national resources, and abundant streams of revenue gushed forth. He touched the dead corpse of public credit, and it sprung upon its feet." That "dead corpse" is worthy of Jefferson's "false facts."

Nevertheless, Jefferson wrote that Hamilton had duped him at his own dinner table, "making him a tool for forwarding his schemes, not then sufficiently understood by me." One suspects that Jefferson knew pretty much what Hamilton was up to, even in the matter of the Bank of the United States, extraconstitutional as it was. Certainly the placing of the District of Columbia in fairly close proximity to the mansions of Washington, Madison, and Jefferson must have made very good sense to him, although Abraham Lincoln, years later, may well have cursed his three great predecessors for placing the capital at the heart of the Confederacy, with Virginia to one side and secession-minded Maryland to the other. But who could have known? In fact, one of the ongoing puzzles of history is: who knew what when?

In 1790 Spain was interfering with British shipping. Each side would presumably pay for American assistance or, at the very least, neutrality. How to negotiate? Normally the secretary of state would, through his envoys to the two countries, put forward interesting terms. But did he know then that his Anglophile rival Hamilton, de facto premier to the president, was English Secret Agent Number Seven? Did he know that his future vice president—now Senator Aaron Burr—was a French agent for the Directory at Paris? Did he know then what was later revealed at the time of Burr's trial for treason, that the commanding general of the American army, James Wilkinson, was for years an agent of the principal land enemy of the United States, Spain?

In *Anas* he makes no reference to these . . . lobbyists, to use a current word for those who profit from unpatriotic activities undertaken for domestic and foreign masters. During the English-Spanish crisis, Hamilton received a fellow agent of the British crown, Major George Beckwith, aide to the governor-general of Canada. Whatever was decided between them, Hamilton then met with Washington, in Jefferson's presence, and spoke of the desirability of an alliance with England against Spain.

Jefferson saw the potential trap. Should England take over the Floridas and Louisiana, "Instead of two neighbors balancing each other, we shall have one, with more than the strength of both."

Unknown to Jefferson, the King's Privy Council for Trade (April 17, 1790) had reported, "It will be for the benefit of the country to prevent Vermont and Kentucky and all the other settlements now forming in the interior . . . from becoming dependent on the government of the US." Jefferson appears to have suspected just what was in train and so urged the administration to assure Spain of its neutrality if Louisiana and Florida were granted independence. To this end, Jefferson had already dispatched an envoy to Madrid.

Meanwhile, British Agent Number Seven was fulfilling more than his job as Great Britain's man on the spot. He warned Beckwith that the pro-French Jefferson could make trouble "from some opinions he has given respecting your government," but, luckily, "Washington was perfectly dispassionate." Then Hamilton appears to divide his loyalties: "I shall certainly know the progress of negotiations from day to day. . . . In case any such difficulties should occur, I should wish to know them in order that I may be sure they are clearly understood and candidly examined." A double agent appears to have been born. By December 1791 Jefferson realized that Hamilton was leaking the content of cabinet meetings to the British. By 1792 the rivals were so at odds that Washington came down from his Olympus and asked each what this great division in his cabinet—now being reflected in the nation—was all about.

On September 8, 1792, Jefferson put pen to paper: "From the moment at which history can stoop to notice [Hamilton], is a tissue of machinations against the liberty of the country which has not only received and given him bread but heaped its honors on his head." This is very much *de haut en bas* for so great a democrat as Jefferson. He does not mention the core of his mistrust, which was Hamilton's view of himself not only as premier to the king, but for his meddling in foreign affairs. Did Jefferson know about Agent Number Seven? Probably not. Certainly, if he had known, he would have toppled Hamilton. Although Hamilton's financial system was primarily intended to increase the credit of the United States in the world, he seemed not to know—or acknowledge, if he knew—that U.S. credit was quite high at Paris and Amsterdam, thanks to the work of ambassadors Adams and Jefferson. Aside from land, the United States' essential source of wealth was farm surplus. Hamilton wanted domestic manufactures to be central so that the republic could exchange with Europe on equal terms. Also, "tis for the United States to consider by what means they can render themselves least dependent on the combinations, right or wrong, of foreign policy." It is curious how often subtle antagonists tend—unthinkingly?—to agree.

The war between the rivals suddenly went public. Pseudonymously, Hamilton wrote for his Federalist newspaper and Jefferson got others (chiefly Madison) to write for his Republican newspaper *Aurora*. A nation that had started without political parties was now dividing itself between Hamiltonian Federalists and Jeffersonian Republicans, or, as Hamilton noted to Washington, "Mr. Madison cooperating with Mr. Jefferson . . . at the head of a faction decidedly hostile to me and my administration. Jefferson and Madison were in my judgment subversive of the principles of good government and dangerous to the union, peace and happiness of the country."

Washington's anger was a slow but certain force once ignited. He rebuked both men: for allowing "internal dissensions" that harrow and tear our vitals. Privately, he told Jefferson that he must show "more charity for the opinions and acts of another." He warned Hamilton about his volatile temper as well as his penchant for rushing into print with "irritating charges." He urged each to make "allowances, mutual forbearances and temporizing, yielding *on all sides.*" Plainly, the father of his country knew best, but his intransigent sons ignored him.

Washington had only one card left to play. He would *not* be a candidate for reelection in 1792. With age, he was becoming more than ever thin-skinned to personal attacks in the press. He was certainly sick of his two warring ministers. But his threat not to run again did catch their attention. Each begged him (as did almost everyone else) to serve a second term. With his habitual air of reluctance, President Washington allowed the grateful people of a newly politicized polity to elect him president unanimously in the Electoral College, with John Adams yet again *in esse* nothing but *in posse* everything . . . maybe.

Five

The second term of President Washington gave no one involved much pleasure. The French Revolution continued to hold the Republicans in thrall. In Boston Francophiles addressed each other—presumably in English with Boston accents—Citizen and Citizeness and called loudly for the death of all aristocrats even though New England notoriously lacked any such order. In 1793 the new French republic sent a raw young polemicist as minister to the United States, Edmond Charles Genet, who insisted that the United States honor the Franco-American treaty of 1778, which pledged each country to come to the aid of the other in the event of war. Luckily for the administration's doves, the treaty meant assistance only in a defensive war. Since, in this case, France was clearly the aggressor, Washington came to the aid of no one. He personally proclaimed a policy of neutrality in this latest European war. He also, daringly, forgot to consult Congress. Genet wanted Washington to confront him before Congress assembled. Washington set about getting the French to recall him.

John Adams had known Genet's family in France: he had also known the boy himself. Politely, he received the fiery minister and then wrapped him round with Adamsian analysis of the graveyard sort: "A youth totally destitute of all experience in popular government, popular assemblies, or conventions of any kind: very little accustomed to reflect upon his own or his fellow creatures' hearts; wholly ignorant of the law of nature and nations . . . " Adams did grant him "a declamatory style . . . a flitting, fluttering imagination, an ardor in his temper, and a civil deportment." Thus two centuries ago the witty French had sent us an archetypal personality whose American avatar would one day be placed in Washington's by now rickety chair.

Jefferson, who was romantically prepared to receive France's gift to Republican America, also quarreled, yet again, with Hamilton, who felt that to receive this ambassador from a murderous republic would amount to recognition of the Terror and, worse, bind us to the treaty of 1778. Jefferson won this round, to his regret. Jefferson's ultimate epitaph for Genet: "hotheaded, all imagination, no judgment, passionate, disrespectful, and even indecent toward the President." Meanwhile, Agent Number Seven was confiding all of this to the British minister George Hammond, who doubtless took heart when he realized that there would be no war between the United States and England but, very likely, one between the United States and the French republic. By and large, outplayed by Hamilton at court, Jefferson retired as secretary of state at the end of 1793 and went home to Monticello.

Adams wrote Abigail "that I have for so long been in an habit of thinking well of his abilities and general good dispositions that I cannot but feel some regret at this event." But Adams could not for long sustain the hypocritical or, perhaps, divided note. Since Adams himself was candid, often to the point of folly, he complains of Jefferson's "want of candor, his obstinate prejudices both of aversion and attachment; his real partiality in spite of his pretension, and his low notions about many things have so nearly reconciled me to it that I will not weep."

Adams did not for a moment believe that Jefferson had forsaken public life. Quite the contrary. "Instead of being the ardent pursuer of science that some think him, he is indolent and his soul is poisoned with ambition." Adams would be the first to admit that it takes, as they say, one to know one. Piously, he hoped that, once free of the vice presidency, he could rid himself of the "foul fiend ambition." Meanwhile, he was preparing to be successor to Washington should the great man choose not to run a third time.

As for the farmer at Monticello, "I am almost tempted to wish he may be chosen Vice-president at the next election." Of that post Adams had written several months earlier: "My country has in its wisdom contrived for me the most insignificant office that was the invention of man . . . or his imagination conceived; and as I can do neither good nor evil, I must be borne away by others and meet the common fate." Adams does enjoy brooding on Jefferson's character or lack of it. Jefferson spent too much money on living well. Perhaps, he left office because he "could not subdue his pride and vanity as I have done," this vainglorious sentiment is confided to his brilliant son John Quincy, who, alone at times, could see the bright nimbus of sainthood that enveloped his rotundity's cherubic form. "Ambition," declares the saint to his heir, "is the subtlest beast of the intellectual and moral field. It is wonderfully adroit in concealing itself from its owner, I had almost said from itself. Jefferson thinks by this step to get a reputation of an humble, modest, meek man wholly without ambition or vanity. He may even have deceived himself into this belief. But if a prospect opens, the world will see and he will feel that he is as ambitious as Oliver Cromwell though no soldier." This last was a dig at Jefferson's having fled, when governor of Virginia, from a British army.

Jefferson himself could tolerate contradictions such as his ongoing fear of the ultimate effects of slavery on the American people so at odds with his daily acceptance of it. He did believe, of course, that reasonable men could sort out any and perhaps every problem. Finally, a child of the Enlightenment, he thought that should reason reign, the pursuit of happiness might yet end in its capture.

Adams was of Manichean disposition. All that was truly human was, to him, truly flawed. Sin, whether original or unoriginal and imposed by circumstance, made human progress a slow, perhaps impossible, business. Paradoxically, a later generation of pagan-minded American fundamentalists chose to place an image of the optimist Jefferson on a Dakota cliff, alongside the father of the gods, the renewer of the Union and the protoimperialist, quite ignoring the truly American Adams, who represented the tortured conscience of a nation sprung from bewitched soil, prone to devil belief and, lately, to bloody wars against serpentine evil everywhere, forever wriggling its way through sacred gardens.

Although Adams possessed a belligerent nature, he was no war lover. When the Senate decided the time had come to teach Algiers a lesson in the Mediterranean for its attacks on American shipping, Adams broke a tie-vote—for peace. He was more than willing to fight for American rights, but as of 1794, in the absence of an army and navy, any such enterprise seemed to him uncommonly feckless. In this, he was as one with Washington, whose Proclamation of Neutrality was a notification for jingo Americans as well as for predatory foreigners. The United States was not yet equipped for foreign wars and so there would be none until the foreign debts had been paid off and there was money to build ships to fight Algerine pirates off the shores of Tripoli and, if necessary, the French and the English. Adams preached reason to his unruly charges, the Senate. Privately, he did not contemplate them with much respect. "It is to be sure a punishment to hear other men talk five hours every day, and not be at liberty to talk at all myself, especially as more than half I hear appears to me very young, inconsiderate and inexperienced."

A new French minister soothed relations with that republic. Now it was the British turn to make trouble. Since American ships serviced French islands in the Caribbean, a British fleet entered the Caribbean and hijacked 250 American ships. Adams was in despair at this latest folly on the part of what Abigail called that "mad and unjust nation." It also brought on an Adamsian fit of prescience. He agreed with Abigail that "Britain has done much amiss and deserves all that will fall thereon." He also saw likeness in British madness to that of the United States, which was "her very image and superscription . . . as true a gamecock as she and, I warrant you, shall become as great a scourge to mankind."

The fifth year of the American constitutional republic should have been a time of consolidation, as well as enjoyment of certain aspects of Hamilton's financial system. But the French-English-Spanish wars stirred up the lobbyists of those countries and set off many a coffeehouse row. A renewed war with England was very much a possibility, even though, as Adams noted, the ones who supported such a war were equally opposed to increasing the budget to pay for it. Madison, whose sense of humor was of the deadpan sort, suggested to the hotheads of the House of Representatives that we might successfully prosecute such a war if the Portuguese would let us hire their fleet. The House did not take up this imaginative proposition; instead they voted for the building of six frigates and a suspension of all commerce with England. Adams realized that should the Senate pass this nonintercourse bill, there would be war. Once again there was a tie-vote; once again he voted for peace.

Washington thought it time to negotiate with England. Hamilton proposed that Chief Justice John Jay go to London. The anti-Federalist Republicans wanted war. Many of them, particularly the Virginians, owed money to England, debts they hoped a war would cancel. Adams had often complained that Jefferson's antipathy to England was due to his personal indebtedness. Jay's mild treaty pleased no one. Although Jefferson had pronounced himself out of politics, he denounced that Jay treaty as an "infamous act, which is really nothing more than a treaty of alliance with the Anglomen of this country against the legislature and people of the United States." Meanwhile, Washington's 1793 unilateral Proclamation of Neutrality was made law by Congress.

When a number of Pennsylvania farmers refused to pay an excise tax on whiskey, federal agents tried to force them to pay. The agents were met with armed resistance. For Washington this Whiskey Rebellion was Shays's rebellion all over again. He must now, like Hotspur, summon his troops. But would they come?

Indeed, *where* were they? State militias tend to the incorporeal. Washington became even more alarmed when he realized that there was a growing tax revolt in Maryland, Georgia, the Carolinas. There was also talk of a march on Philadelphia. When the president ordered the insurgents to disperse, the nightmare of every commander came true. They did not obey.

The father of the nation drew his sword, ascended the throne, and commanded the nation to forthwith provide twelve thousand men to put down the rebellion. Americans finally came to their senses. More than twelve thousand men rallied around Washington, who, with Hamilton at his side, rode straight to the heart of the rebellion in western Pennsylvania where twenty no doubt deeply embarrassed moonshiners surrendered; recanted; and received a presidential pardon. Hamilton headed back to New York to prepare for the election of 1796.

Washington did not mean to be a candidate for a third term, but, wise in the ways of the world, he was not about to make a definite statement until the last moment: lame ducks cannot soar like eagles and, at any moment, in so raw and anarchic a republic, he needed at least the appearance of an eagle to maintain order. Even so, those close to him were very much aware how the presidency had worn him down. He had been particularly outraged by press criticism, much of it the work of new arrivals from Ireland and England gifted in all the arts of libel: and quite aware that wild attacks upon the greatest American would gain them maximum attention.

Adams suffered many a mood change during 1796. He expected to be the choice of the Federalists just as Jefferson would be the choice of the Republicans. But. There was disturbing talk that Patrick Henry and Hamilton might be candidates; the first subtracting votes from Jefferson; the second from Adams.

The campaign began February 10 in the Republican newspaper *Aurora*, which admonished the States' electors to choose the "good patriot, statesman and philosopher" Thomas Jefferson. Adams promptly vowed to Abigail, "I am determined to be a silent spectator of the silly and wicked game, and to enjoy it as a comedy, a farce, or a gymnastic exhibition at Sadler's Wells." This lightness of tone showed how worried he was; yet, surely, he had overcome *mere* ambition. Certainly, it was in a mood of serene selflessness that he wrote Thomas Jefferson an amiable letter. Sounding out his rival? Heaven forbid. They were two disinterested philosophers, meditating on public affairs, *pro bono publico*.

Adams deplored the excesses of the French Revolution, for the record? Delicately, he probed Jefferson's most vulnerable spot. Of course, when it came to the higher hypocrisy no Adams could ever outmatch the lord of Monticello. Jefferson, aside from farming, was now using his slaves to manufacture nails. He was much too busy for politics, "a subject I never loved," he writes, "and now hate." Thus, he aced Adams. Jefferson admitted that the constantly changing regimes in Paris were of a disturbing "oligarchical nature," then, anticipating Adams's return, he gave a splendid spin to the ball: "I am sure from the honesty of your heart, you join me in detestation of the corruption of the English government, and that no man on earth is more incapable than yourself of seeing that copied among us willingly." In other words, you play the French card and I will play the English card. Not a satisfying rally for Adams.

Washington and Adams, socially at least, were growing closer. With Jefferson and Hamilton gone from his cabinet, the president was more than ever isolated. Only Adams, of the original creators, remained. To Abigail he wrote, "Yesterday the President sent his carriage for me to go with the family to the theater. *The Rage* and *The Spoiled Child* were the two pieces. It rained and the house was not full." There is an implication that when the president went out in public, he rather fancied a large cheering crowd. In any event, he appeared "worried and growing old faster than I could wish and his lady complains of infirmities of age and lowness of spirit for the first time."

Washington had every reason to be worried. The Jay treaty was before the House of Representatives, and the Republicans were bent on its destruction, as well as of the Federalist Party and, to Adams's alarmed eye, of the republic itself. Should they succeed in their destructiveness, "It will be then evident that this constitution cannot stand. . . . If the House of Representatives condemn the treaty and defeat its operation, I see nothing but the dissolution of government and immediate war. President, Senate and House all dissolve and an old Congress revives, debts are all cancelled, paper money issued and forced into circulation by the bayonets, and, in short, heaven and earth set at defiance." In the end the treaty was accepted; and Adams headed for Quincy to await that selection of electors in the various States which would decide his fate.

He vacillated between indifference to the presidency and a conviction that he alone in that office could prevent any number of wars. Yet he did not think it quite the end of the world if Jefferson was elected. "Be sober," he admonished himself. "Be calm, oh, my heart, and let your temperance and moderation be known to all men."

Between 1793 and 1797 the farmer-philosopher Jefferson seems to have undergone what a later generation would term a midlife crisis, to which he alludes, April 27, 1795, in a letter to Madison, the acknowledged leader of the Republican Party, whose idol was—Jefferson himself. "My health," he writes Madison, "is entirely broken down within the last eight months." Yet at fifty, he was not about to relinquish his web of political operatives while, simultaneously, building and rebuilding Monticello and farming (wheat—not tobacco). Of this curious period, he later writes to his daughter Polly, "From 1793 to 1797, I remained closely at home, saw none but those who came there, and at length became very sensible of the ill effect it had upon my own mind, and of its direct and irresistible tendency to render unfit for society, and uneasy when necessarily engaged in it. I felt enough of the effect of withdrawing from the world then, to see that it led to an anti-social and misanthropic state of mind, which severely punishes him who gives in to it." Although for thirty-seven months Jefferson never strayed more than seven miles from Monticello, he wrote letters, read newspapers, received visitors. One year after he had settled into his "retirement," Madison was putting him forward as Republican candidate for president against "the British party."

Alexander Hamilton had resigned as secretary of the treasury January 31, 1795, a Saturday; on the following Monday, Washington accepted the resignation, coolly: "In every relation which you have borne to me, I have found that my confidence in your talents, exertions and integrity has been well placed." On February 3 Hamilton replied, "As often as I may recall the vexations I have endured, your approbation will be a great and precious consolation. You will always have my fervent wishes for your public and private felicity."

In politics mutual need, no matter how temporary, is all that matters. For the moment, Hamilton was now free to return to New York City, to the law, to his compulsive political conniving, and he would not return until the president needed him for one final task; the composition of the president's Farewell to the Nation, a sort of credo which would prove to be, after the extraordinary insight that a national debt, properly administered, is the secret of national wealth, Hamilton's (and Washington's) enduring legacy to the American system. Washington's original cabinet was, finally, dispersed except for Edmund Randolph, now secretary of state.

In London, John Jay had concluded a treaty with England which Lord Grenville and he had signed. But as of March 4, the day that Congress adjourned, no copy of the treaty had arrived, making it impossible for the Senate to give or withhold its advice and consent. Washington and Randolph were rightly nervous as to the treaty's contents.

Finally, on March 7, "The Treaty of *Amity, Commerce and Navigation*" arrived, accompanied by Jay's bleak note to Washington: "It must speak for itself. . . . To do more was not possible." What the treaty said for itself was that England had achieved a considerable diplomatic victory, largely thanks to British Agent Seven, who had carefully undermined Jay's bargaining points by passing on to London a preview of the American positions. Presumably, Hamilton's often-avowed fear of war with England led him to sell, as it were, the pass. In July 1794 Hamilton had met with his spymaster, George Hammond, the British minister at Philadelphia, and told him many things that the Foreign Office in London needed to know. For instance, the threat that the United States would, if thwarted by His Majesty's government, make a military alliance with the Baltic states was never on the cards. In a further dotting of I's and crossing of T's, Hamilton assured Hammond (who then assured Lord Grenville) that under no circumstances would Washington's administration combine with any other European power. Hammond wrote the Foreign Office that Hamilton had said, "with great seriousness and with every demonstration of sincerity, that it was the settled policy of this government in every contingency, even in that of an open contest with Great Britain, to avoid entangling itself with European connections." Thus Lord Grenville was forewarned of Jay's best stratagems.

At a point like this in a fictional narrative, there would be a confrontation between Washington and Hamilton. From what we know of each man, and each armed with this particular information, the dramatist could move if not into Shakespeare land (Brutus and Cassius at Philippi), then at least into Schiller's *Mary Stuart*, where the Queen of Scots denounces the Queen of England to her face as, literally, a bastard—like Hamilton. But no record in actual history is seldom so completed; hence, swarms of bees are constantly, and most usefully, forever abuzz in Academe's hives.

As Congress did not reconvene until a special session, June 8, Washington could keep the treaty all afire in his pocket and say nothing. In the second of the treaty's twenty-eight articles, England pledged to evacuate its western posts, but not until June 1796. Other articles vaguely took into account American maritime losses due to English assaults on American shipping, but article eighteen was arrogantly blunt: in England's current war with France, England asserted its right to seize any food and provisions as contraband of war. A wet spring was endangering England's winter wheat crop.

George Washington went home to Mount Vernon, to wait for Jay's return. Let Jay explain his treaty to the Senate. The president would not.

Once on his home ground, Washington could make plans for the federal city that would bear his name. An interesting bee in *his* bonnet was the necessity for a future world capital (if he so thought of it) to be home to an important university. He addressed the city's commissioners: "It has always been a source of serious reflection and sincere regret with me that the youth of the United States should be sent to foreign countries for the purpose of education. For this reason, I have greatly wished to see a plan adopted by which the arts, sciences and belles letters could be taught in their fullest extent." If such a plan were to go forward, he would contribute the famous fifty shares of the Potomac Company that he had, so many years before, accepted with the public proviso that he might someday give them to a worthy cause. Meanwhile, in the matter of education, he wrote a friend searching for proper American schools. The General suggested Massachusetts, where "order, regularity and a prompt regard to morals, in and out of school, is very much attended to. And, besides, Harvard College near Boston is at hand for the completion of education . . . and is, I am told in high repute." On the other hand, when John Adams suggested that the University of Geneva be transported to the United States, Washington wondered just "how far any *entire* seminary of *foreigners*, who may not understand our language, can be assimilated."

The repercussions of Jay's treaty resonated for a long time. John Jay himself had given up the chief justiceship of the United States in order to put at risk the Federalist cause by signing a treaty carefully sabotaged by the leader of the Federalist faction. Hamilton, for his part, may have sincerely felt that by accommodating England in the Twenty-Eight Articles he could prevent war with *his* most favored nation as well as harm, somehow, John Adams in the process. Jay, while abroad, had been elected governor of New York in the Federalist interest, which theoretically made him a great player in national politics, but the general storm over his treaty ended any hope of national leadership. After two terms as New York's governor, John Jay retired from public life.

The treaty barely passed the Senate. Arguably, it avoided an immediate war with England while infuriating the French, a people whose nation was being reorganized by its brilliant young general Napoleon Bonaparte. Jay's treaty might easily have been more advantageous to the United States had he been aware of England's mounting troubles. Due to mutinies within the famous fleet, the British navy in November 1796 abandoned the Mediterranean, thus tempting Bonaparte to conquer, briefly, Egypt.

One of the oddities of American history was the fascination that Bonaparte's career had for so many of our "republican" leaders. As he swept across Europe, winning military victory after victory, not to mention crowning himself Emperor of the French in the process, his two most enthralled American admirers were, like him, five-foot-seven or so, like him, soldiers: Lieutenant Colonel Aaron Burr, boy-hero of the invasion of Canada, and Major General Alexander Hamilton, victor of the war against Pennsylvania's moonshiners. Also, oddly, when neither Hamilton nor Burr was politically viable in the republic any longer, each made connection with Latin-American revolutionaries in the hopes of finding for himself a Napoleonic throne, preferably in Mexico. Napoleon had made it all look so easy. Ironically, while young Frenchmen like the Marquis de Lafayette dreamed of emulating George Washington, at least two youngish Americans were bedazzled by Napoleon and his Marlovian conquests. Finally, the two were, at some level, so alike that one killed the other in a duel. The survivor, Burr, lived to a great old age, practicing law in New York City. Of the duel with his rival he remarked cryptically, "Had I read Voltaire less and Sterne more, I might have thought the world wide enough for Hamilton and me."

Jay's Treaty not only proved to be the beginning of the end for the Federalist Party but also put at risk Adams's election as successor to Washington. Inevitably, furor over the treaty gave a great impetus to the Republicans and to the philosopher-king on his hilltop at Monticello, where he orchestrated the Republican end of the pseudonymous debates in the newspapers, themselves the principal bloody battleground for argument and counter-argument, not to mention the higher libels. But the eloquent Jefferson did not, himself, write. He usually got the loyal wise Madison to do his arguing for him. Hamilton, on the other hand, wielded the fastest, most dazzling pen in the republic.

Washington, always so far above the battle that he often saw everything more clearly than others, wrote Hamilton on July 29, 1795,

> The cry against the treaty is like that against a mad dog; and everyone, in a manner, seems engaged in running it down. It has received the most tortured interpretation. . . . The string which is most played on, because it strikes with most force the popular ear, is the violation, as they term it, of our engagements with France, or, in other words, the predilection shown to Great Britain at the expense of the French nation. . . . It is the interest of the French to avail themselves of such a spirit to keep *us* and *Great Britain* at variance. . . . To what *length* their policy may induce them to carry matters is too much in embryo at this moment to decide. But I predict much embarrassment to the govern-ment therefrom, and . . . too much pains cannot be taken, by those who speak or write in favor of the treaty.

The president is now writing a fan letter. He has just seen a piece that Hamilton had written in a New York (Republican!) paper, *Argus*, July 22, 1795. Hamilton, as "Camillus," was to write, serially, twenty-two pieces and later six more. John Jay also wrote as "Camillus," as did Senator Rufus King of New York.

Hamilton's wide-ranging defense of the treaty and the perils—like civil war—that it would avert, so alarmed Jefferson that he wrote his lawyer (that is, Madison): "Hamilton is really a colossus to the anti-republican party. He is a host within himself. We have had only middling performances to oppose him. In truth, when he comes forward, there is nobody but yourself who can meet him. For God's sake, take up your pen and give a fundamental reply." The storm over the treaty continued with Hamilton, at its center, ensuring for himself the de facto leadership of the Federalist Party.

While General Washington was home in Virginia, meeting with the directors of the Potomac Company at Alexandria, his cabinet, now peopled by the second-rate and worse, was aboil with plots and counter-plots. On July 31 the secretary of war, Timothy Pickering, wrote a letter urging the president to hurry back to Philadelphia: "On the subject of the treaty I confess that I feel extreme solicitude. I pray you to decide on no important political measure in whatever form it may be presented to you. This letter is for your eye alone." Simultaneously, Secretary of State Randolph, who had just written the president to stay put, that all was well, now wrote, at Pickering's urging, that he should return. This was enough to put the affairs of the Potomac Company on the back burner. Washington headed north. What was happening?

Pickering, in combination with the secretary of the treasury, Oliver Wolcott, a fellow New Englander and Hamiltonian, favored the treaty, while Secretary Randolph insisted on modifications. Upon arrival in Philadelphia, Washington dined with Randolph; and sent for Pickering. When the secretary of war arrived, Washington, glass of wine in hand, motioned for Pickering to join him in the next room.

Once alone, Washington asked Pickering, "What is the cause of your writing me such a letter?"

This is Pickering's version, years later, of what happened. He writes that he indicated the dining room door, "That man is a traitor," he said. Washington, as cliché still has it, was struck dumb. Apparently, the British minister, Hammond, had received from London some intercepted correspondence of the French minister, Fauchet. As of October 31, 1792, Secretary of State Randolph had appeared to ask for a bribe from the French in return for his good offices.

Apparently, the President, a master of himself if not his associates, absorbed this information in silence. "Let us return to the other room," he said. Presently, the two secretaries took their leave. Later, Secretary Wolcott presented the president with Fauchet's dispatch number ten as clumsily translated by Pickering with the help of a French grammar. The most striking line was "Besides, the precious confessions of Mr. Randolph alone throw a satisfactory light upon everything that comes to light." In context "precious confessions" appears to mean state secrets. If true, the secretary of state had indeed committed treason. Was it likely? In the matter of Jay's treaty, he had been even-handed in dealing with France and England: he favored ratification with English modifications. If these dispatches are indeed genuine, Pickering, their translator, scored a number of points that would have set the president's elaborately crafted teeth on edge: Randolph in paragraph fourteen observes of recent moves by what seems like some sort of cabal "that under pretexts of giving energy to the government, it was intended to introduce absolute power and to mislead the President in paths which would conduct him to unpopularity." The whiskey rebellion?

Then, Fauchet continued,

Three men, with others unknown to me, all having without doubt Randolph at their head, were balancing to decide upon their party. Mr. Randolph came to see me with a countenance expressive of much anxiety, and made to me the overtures of which I have given you an account in my No. 6 [not available to Washington]. Thus with some thousands of dollars the [French] republic would have decided on civil war or on peace. Thus the consciences of the pretended patriots of America have already their scale of prices! . . . What will be the old age of this government, if it is thus early decrepit! Such, Citizen, is the evident consequence of the system of finances conceived by Mr. Hamilton. He has made a whole nation a stock-jobbing, speculating, selfish people. Riches alone here fix consideration.

Francophobes in our time should be deeply annoyed at so unfriendly a description of the genesis of the great American formula: socialism for the rich, free enterprise for the poor. But was Randolph's "treason" true? Was Fauchet's Englished dispatch—in which he refers to Jefferson, Madison, and Monroe as "honest patriots"—his?

Washington would have been even more in the dark about all this than we. He had known Pickering and Wolcott from the Revolution. But Randolph was of the same Virginia family as he. Washington also knew that Randolph had an invalid wife, a large family, no money. The president was more than ever isolated, even, perhaps, irrelevant. The machine whose engine he had started seemed stalled. Dutifully, he made a précis of Fauchet's material.

Later, Pickering, in his published *Miscellaneous Notes* (1826), writes that in cabinet only Randolph, unaware of the plot against him, did not want the treaty ratified as long as England refused to revise the offending articles on contraband. The others wanted instant ratification. Finally, Washington rose and said, "I will ratify the treaty." And that was that.

August 1795 was not a high moment in the republic's history. On August 19 Washington, in front of Pickering and Wolcott, gave Randolph an intercepted letter from Fauchet to Paris. In silence, Randolph read the letter in which he appears to be offering to sell state secrets to the French. When Randolph tried to explain the letter, Washington indicated that Pickering and Wolcott should question their colleague; and left the room. That afternoon Randolph resigned. To Washington, he wrote, "Your confidence in me, Sir, has been unlimited and I can truly affirm, unabused. My sensations then, cannot be concealed when I find that confidence so immediately withdrawn, without a word or distant hint being previous dropped to me." In December of that year, Randolph wrote *A Vindication* of himself. Meanwhile, Pickering replaced him as secretary of state (the object of the exercise?). There is an immense amount of puzzled and puzzling scholarly analysis of this business. The one conclusion that most historians agree upon is that Timothy Pickering, false or true, was a terrible translator from French to English.

In 1792 Washington had asked Madison to prepare him a Farewell Address that, as it turned out, he did not need to deliver because he chose to serve a second term. In preparation for going home on March 4, 1796, the president had composed his own version of the Farewell, retaining ten paragraphs from Madison's text. Since Madison was now, in effect, the head of the Republican Party, Washington turned to Hamilton for the "public annunciation of his retirement." Hamilton doubtless saw the possibilities of incorporating in such a document as much as possible of his own brand of Federalism. The president sent him the Washington-Madison text, with a note, "Even if you should think it best to throw the whole into a different form, let me request . . . that my draught may be returned . . . curtailed if too verbose, and relieved of all tautology; my wish is that the whole may appear in a plain style and be handed to the public in an honest unaffected, simple garb." After a lifetime spent making history and speaking historically, Washington was very much aware that the high historical form of address tends to bottom itself upon tautology; his "real life" conversation, if he could be said to have had much, tended to uninformative brevity. Visitors found him disappointingly uncommunicative, but then he realized that whenever a stranger showed up at Mount Vernon, the president was bound to be quoted—and, such is the way of the world, dangerously misquoted. As it proved, Hamilton's original draft pleased the president; there was also a draft for incorporation with the original, but Washington settled on the original, in which his own sometimes querulous text betrayed, at moments, an almost Adamsian self-pity which Hamilton with his ever-dexterous feather gloriously marbleized.

In September 1796 Washington's Farewell was released to the national press. With this document, the third presidential election began. Certainly, the Farewell can be seen as a defense of Federalism, but Hamilton, in Thucydidean mode, knew that he was writing in the style of a great man—above petty politics, eye always upon the future of his country and threatening dangers upon the horizon. The beginning is spacious.

The period for a new election of a Citizen, to Administer the Executive government of the United States, being not far distant . . . the strength of my desire to withdraw previous to the last election, had even led to the preparation of an address to declare it to you, but deliberate reflection on the very critical and perplexed posture of our affairs with foreign nations, and the unanimous advice of men every way entitled to my confidence, obliged me to abandon the idea.

The impressions, under which, I first accepted the arduous trust of Chief Magistrate, were explained on the proper occasion. In the discharge of this trust, I can only say, that I have, with pure intentions, contributed towards the organization and administration of the government, the best exertions of which a very fallible judgment was capable.

Washington emphasizes the importance of the Union and warns of sectional rivalries—West versus East, North versus South: "All the parts of our country will find in their union strength. and what is more valuable, an exemption from those broils and wars between the parts if disunited which, then, our rivalships, fomented by foreign intrigue or the opposite alliances with foreign nations engendered [by] their mutual jealousies, would inevitably produce."

Washington next warns of "the petulance of party." In the margin, Hamilton prefers the phrase the "collisions and disgusts of
party." Hamilton does not seem to have had much taste for irony.
If he had, he might have enjoyed how *his* George is, in Hamiltonian prose, warning in such powerful terms against party bick-
ering and maneuvering of the sort that Hamilton was now whole-
heartedly using in secret against his own party's candidate for
president. In 1789 he had kept Adams from getting a majority of
the electoral votes for vice president, weakening him politically.
Now Hamilton, deploring at least in the margin of a manuscript
"collisions and disgusts" of the sort that he himself was arrang-
ing, had put in motion, presumably unknown to the president,
a plan for New England Federalist electors (each had two votes)
to vote unanimously for Adams and Pinckney of South Carolina
while the electors of South Carolina would cast all their votes
for Pinckney as vice president while throwing away a few votes
from Adams. If this plan played out, Pinckney would be president
and Adams, again, vice president. But one potential "disgust" for
Hamilton was the possibility that this maneuver could well result
in the election of the Republicans Jefferson and Aaron Burr as
president and vice president.

Like Adams, Jefferson made no overt moves to gain the presidency. He was even on record that Adams, older than he, able
and honorable, deserved election. Meanwhile, Jefferson insisted
that Madison give him a weekly report on the campaign though
the "little spice of ambition which I had in my younger days has

long since evaporated." This was coy. He was certainly not well-pleased when the new French minister, Adet, did everything but stump for him on the ground that only Jefferson could avert a war with France.

New England Federalists, forewarned of Hamilton's plot, did not vote for Pinckney. On the other hand, South Carolina's electors followed the Hamiltonian plan, giving Pinckney and Jefferson eight votes each, which brought Jefferson to within three votes of Adams, thus making him a most unlikely Republican vice president to the new Federalist President Adams.

While setting in motion these collisions and disgusts, Hamilton concluded his great aria for Washington. The president warns of the dangers of the three branches of government impinging upon each other. "The spirit of encroachment tends to absorb the powers of the several branches and departments into one and thus to establish, under whatever forms, a despotism. A just knowledge of the human heart, of that love of power which predominates in it . . . "—here Hamilton drops the Washingtonian mask and speaks as Iago, who so famously said, "You know what you know"—" . . . is alone sufficient to establish this truth. Let there be no change by usurpation, for though this may be the instrument of good in one instance, it is the ordinary instrument of the destruction of free government," as we now daily witness two centuries later.

Both Hamilton and Washington are as one in their fear of the stratagems of foreign nations in their wars which so often tended to embroil America. Washington prefers his prose formulation to that of Hamilton who wrote, marginally, "It is very material that while we entertain proper impressions of particular cases of friendly or unfriendly conduction of different foreign nations towards us, we nevertheless avoid fixed and rooted antipathies against any, or passionate attachments for any, instead of these cultivating, as a general rule, just and amicable feelings towards all."

Washington's text was looser:

Nothing is more essential than that antipathies against particular nations and passionate attachments for others should be avoided and that instead of them we should cultivate just and amicable feelings towards all. That nation which indulges towards another an habitual hatred or an habitual fondness, is in some degree a slave. . . . It is a slave to its animosity, or to its affection—either of which is sufficient to lead it astray from its duty and interest. The nation urged by resentment and rage, sometimes compels the government to war, contrary to its own calculations of policy. The government sometimes participates in this propensity and dons through passion what reason would forbid it at other times; it makes the animosity of the nations subservient to hostile projects which originate in ambition and other sinister motives.

Of the two, Washington's version is most applicable to our Union today as the great combine of military, media, religious mania, and lust for oil has overthrown those safeguards that the first three presidents, for all their disagreements, were as one in wishing to preserve, protect, and defend.

Six

At the beginning of December 1796, Vice President Adams returned (from Massachusetts) to the seat of government at Philadelphia. During the autumn, he had gone through many moods, none apparently serene. It is a sign, perhaps, of Adams's trusting if not noble temperament that he had failed to grasp what Hamilton had done to him in the recent election; naturally, he understood that the relatively undistinguished Thomas Pinckney was now a potential president due to some mysterious voting patterns both at the North and at the South. There was much talk that Hamilton and perhaps John Jay were behind this "insidious maneuver" but Adams was also aware that Jefferson's New York political manager, Burr, after delivering New York, had been canvassing votes throughout New England, even spending time in Boston to flatter Adams's radical cousin Sam. Adams's position, whatever the cause of the confusion: if "chance and tricks" were to decide the election, he preferred that either Jefferson or Hamilton win than Pinckney.

In Philadelphia he was received warmly by the General and his lady. It would be interesting to know whether they exchanged hard luck stories. Washington was under fire from the pro-French Republicans, and the French minister Adet was openly interfering in American domestic affairs by speaking out for Jefferson and against the Federalists. Meanwhile, Thomas Paine, the great voice for the American Revolution, had now turned on his onetime hero, Washington. Paine, a Briton turned American, had joined the French Revolution and fallen afoul of the sea-green incorruptible Robespierre, who put him, uncharacteristically, in prison rather than beneath the guillotine. Paine expected Washington to demand that the author of *Common Sense* be freed promptly: he was not—at least not promptly. Always eager to bear a grudge, Paine denounced the president in print as a "patron of fraud" and even a murderer. Why so much fury? Apparently in 1792 Washington had intimated that he would like to read Paine's *Rights of Man*. Paine sent him fifty copies. Did Paine dream of the blurb of blurbs: "Not since the Ten Commandments came to us from Sinai has there been so great, nay, holy a message for all mankind"—*General George Washington, World Hero*. But Washington never acknowledged the gift or made any reference to the text, and so: "As to you, Sir, treacherous in private friendship (for so you have been to me, and that in the day of danger) and a hypocrite in public life, the world will be puzzled to decide, whether you are an apostate or an impostor; whether you have abandoned good principles, or whether you ever had any."

Washington showed Adams a letter in which Paine confides, "I must continue to think you treacherous till you give me cause to think otherwise." Adams wrote Abigail, saying he thought that this letter the weakest "of all Paine's productions."

The Electoral College vote had still to be counted, and at the thought of defeat, John wrote Abigail, "Vanity suffers, cold feelings of unpopularity, humble reflection, mortifications, humiliations, plans of future life. Economy, retrenching of expenses. Farming. Return to the bar. Drawing writs, arguing causes." If he lost the presidency, it must be only to Jefferson or, possibly, Hamilton. Grimly, he wrote Abigail, "The 16 of Feb. will soon come, and then I will take my leave forever. For frugality and independence—poverty and patriotism—love and a carrot bed."

At the very bottom of his distress was the fact that he needed a federal salary. Of course, he could practice law. But could he? after so long away?

When the Senate convened it was Adams's task to reply to Washington's Farewell Address. He did his Roman best to be "firm and cool"; but afterward, he wrote Abigail, "the Senators say I pronounced it in so affecting a manner that I made them cry. The tears certainly did trickle." Washington had trouble with his brief response.

As early as December 28 Jefferson had written Adams, congratulating him on his victory despite the machinations of Hamilton. At that time the only question left was who was to be vice president, Jefferson or Pinckney? Plainly, Jefferson did not lust for this office, but it was now the penultimate step for someone who saw himself as the personification of the people at large who must, in due course, come to power.

It is something of a mystery how Adams, so well acquainted with the principal players in the small world of the early republic, should have found it for so long so hard to believe that Hamilton was forever bent on ridding himself—and the nation—of Adams and his influence. Yet Adams knew better than most how Hamilton had been de facto prime minister to Washington and how he would entirely dominate Pinckney had that unimpressive man been elected. In any case, on February 8 the electoral votes of the States were counted, and Hamilton's machinations did not entirely prevail. Adams won the presidency with seventy-one votes; Jefferson with sixty-eight won the vice presidency. Pinckney got fifty-nine, and Burr, "running mate" to Jefferson, a mere thirty votes.

Adams, as president of the Senate, declared himself to be the president-elect of the United States. From Massachusetts, Abigail was in an "I told you so" mood. Had she not always said,

"Hamilton is as ambitious as Julius Caesar, a subtle intriguer. his thirst for fame is insatiable. I have ever kept my eye upon him."

Adams was now aware that he had been for eight years the victim of a Hamiltonian conspiracy. Yes, he wrote Abigail, he knew "Hamilton to be a proud-spirited, conceited, aspiring mortal, always pretending to morality, with morals as debauched as old Franklin, who is more his model than anyone I know. As great a hypocrite as any in the U.S., his intrigues in the election I despise. That he has 'talents' I admit, but I dread none of them. I shall take no notice of his puppyhood." Adams would "keep him at a distance." Abigail was Shakespearean in her response, "Beware of the spare Cassius, has always occurred to me when I have seen that cock sparrow. Oh, I have read his heart in his wicked eyes many a time. The very devil is in them. They are lasciviousness itself, or I have no skill in physiognomy. Pray burn this letter." In the wised-up twenty-first century, a practitioner of the dark arts and sciences of the mind would say that Abigail, all ablaze, was suffering from an attack of Lady Potiphar's Syndrome.

On March 4, 1797, Washington, dressed in black as a simple citizen, walked to Congress Hall. Despite a sea of bad notices from the Republican press, the departing president was hailed on all sides by the people who were quite aware that someone unique had reigned over them, counseling good relations with all nations. Right to the end, he had the gift of perfect self-presentation. As he approached the door that led to the House of Representatives, the crowd in the street began to cheer. He hurried, modestly, to the door, as befitted a ghost from the past. Once inside the chamber, Washington could hear from the street loud cheering for the new vice president, Thomas Jefferson, as he now mounted the high stage of the national history. In contrast to the slender arthritic former president, he seemed, it was said, mythically tall, in a blue frock coat. Finally, there was applause when the second president of the United States, wearing a pearl-gray suit, a sword, and a cockaded hat, made his entrance and climbed onto the dais and sat in the speaker's chair, flanked to the right by Washington, with Jefferson between them.

Adams rose as the chief justice, Oliver Ellsworth, adjured him to preserve, protect, and defend the Constitution of the United States. As Adams wrote later, "A solemn scene it was indeed, and it was made affecting to me by the presence of the General, whose countenance was as serene and unclouded as the day. He seemed to me to enjoy a triumph over me. Methought I heard him say, 'Ay! I am fairly out and you fairly in! See which of us will be happiest!'"

Inevitably, in those affairs where human vanity is most on view and at its most taut, there is comedy. Once the oath was sworn, Adams gave a short inaugural address, bowed to the chamber, and waddled into history, leaving the great stars behind him on the dais. Washington signaled Jefferson that protocol required that the new vice president must follow his chief in order that they might show themselves to the people. Jefferson, quite aware that the last one out would get the full ovation of the crowd, indicated that the Father of his Country should follow next. But not for nothing had the hero of Valley Forge, of Yorktown, of eight years of Revolution held his ground and always, somehow, got his way. There is no description of either man's face during their ultimate exchange, but it is recorded that Jefferson was obliged to leave the chamber first. Then, slowly, majestically, Washington, having won his last victory in the Mount Rushmore sweepstakes, walked gravely out of the Federal Building and into the wildly cheering crowd, not to mention into the hearts of his countrymen forever. Or until they pretty much forgot him when a later president (and former president of Princeton) decided to conduct a world war in order to make the unsuspecting world "safe for democracy," a word that appears nowhere in the American Constitution, or, indeed, in our lives except as an occasional rhetorical flourish when we are up to mischief in foreign lands.

Although the founders were often good classicists, they took as a model for the American republic the pre–Julius Caesar Roman Republic. For the record, our word *democracy* comes from the Greek *demokratia*, which means, literally, "people-power." History's only democracy was instituted at Athens in 508 B.C. by Cleisthenes. Every male citizen over eighteen years of age was a citizen, able to gather with his fellows on a hillside, where, after listening to various demagogues, he could vote with the other citizens on matters of war and peace and anything else that happened to be introduced that day. In 322 B.C. Alexander of Macedon conquered Athens and eliminated their democracy, which was never again to be tried by a proper state (as opposed to an occasional New England town meeting).

Current publicists for the American Empire have convinced themselves that if other nations, living as they do in utter darkness, would only hold numerous elections at enormous cost to their polity's plutocracy (or to the benign empire back of these exercises), perfect government would henceforward obtain as The People had Been Heard: one million votes for Saddam Hussein, let us say, to five against. Although the Athenian system might now be revived through technology, voting through some sort of "safe" cybersystem, no one would wish an uneducated, misinformed majority to launch a war, much less do something meaningful like balance the budget of Orange County, California.

One interesting aspect of the Athenian system was the rotation of offices. When Pericles told Sophocles, the poet-dramatist, that it was his turn to be postmaster general or some such dull office, Sophocles said he was busy with a play and that, besides, politics was not his business. To which the great Pericles responded, the man who says politics is no business of his has no business.

Much of the significance of December 2000 was that the Electoral College, created to ensure that majority rule be thwarted if unacceptable to what Hamilton thought of as the proper governing elite, threw a bright spotlight on just how undemocratic our republic has become, causing one of the Supreme Court Justices (by many thought to be a visiting alien) to respond to the Gore lawyers who maintained that Florida's skewed voting machines and confused rulings by various interested courts had deprived thousands of Floridians of their vote for president. The American Constitution, said the Justice, mandibles clattering joyously, does not provide *any* American citizen the right to vote for president. This is absolutely true. One votes for a near-anonymous member of the Electoral College, which explains why so few Americans now bother to "vote" for president. But then a majority don't know what the Electoral College is.

Of the inauguration of John Adams, Rufus King wrote: "Mr. Adams is president, Mr. Jefferson is Vice president. Our Jacobins say they are well pleased, and that the *lion* and the lamb are to lie down together. Mr. Adams's personal friends talk a little in the same way. 'Mr. Jefferson is not half so ill a man as we have been accustomed to think him. There is to be a united and a vigorous administration.' Skeptics like me quietly look forward to the event, willing to hope; but not prepared to believe. If Mr. Adams has vanity, 'tis plain a plot has been laid to take hold of it. We trust his real good sense and integrity will be a sufficient shield."

Once the Pinckney maneuver had failed, any hope that Hamilton might have had of acting as prime minister to so seasoned a political player as Adams appeared to be at an end. But Hamilton the intriguant, as Adams called him, was still a power in the land because Adams, out of deference to the departed General, had kept on Washington's cabinet, whose shadow chief was Hamilton. The three great offices of state were held by the cunning mediocrities Pickering, Wolcott, and James McHenry (War), each more or less attached to Hamilton. Not only did this disloyal and incompetent cabinet get the new president off to a bad start but the fact that after so many years away from his home in Quincy, he was determined to spend as much time there as he could and so, between working with his predecessor's second team at a considerable remove in far-off Massachusetts, Adams had, in a sense, removed himself from the actual day-to-day governance of a republic whose affairs were beginning to grow very complex indeed. He did not fully awaken to his situation until 1800, when he was moved into the wilderness of the new capital at Washington.

Adams was not entirely unaware of his situation as early as his investiture. On March 17, 1797, he wrote, "It would have given me great pleasure to have had some of my family present at my inauguration, which was the most affecting and overpowering scene I ever acted in. I was very unwell, had no sleep the night before, and really did not know but I should have fainted in presence of all the world. I was in great doubt whether to say anything or not besides repeating the oath. And now the world is as silent as the grave. All the Federalists seem to be afraid to approve anybody but Washington." An interesting premonition. "The Jacobin papers damn with faint praise, and undermine with misrepresentation and insinuation. If the Federalists go to playing pranks, I will resign the office, and let Jefferson lead them to peace, wealth, and power if he will." A warning to Hamilton's cabal.

> From the situation where I now am, I see a scene of ambition beyond all my former suspicions or imaginations; an emulation which will turn our government topsy-turvy. Jealousies and rivalries have been my theme, and checks and balances their antidotes till I am ashamed to repeat the words; but they never stared me in the face in such horrid forms as at present. I see how the thing is going. At the next elections England will set up Jay or Hamilton, and France, Jefferson and all the corruption of Poland will be introduced; unless the American should rise and say, we will have neither John Bull nor Louis Baboon.

France and Spain were at war with each other while the Anglo-French perennial war was heating up. Vis-à-vis the U.S., the French were suffering from what they affected was *chagrin d'amour*. Once again Americans were reminded, had it not been for the French and their fleet, neither Yorktown nor the Revolution would have been won. As a result, the two nations had been, in effect, married by the treaty of 1783. Later, when it became inconvenient for the U.S. to honor this treaty, it was argued by Washington's government that as it had been between King Louis XVI and the United States, once his monarchy had given way to a medley of exotic governing Directories, Consulates, Republics, the treaty was no longer in force. But despite this quibbling, the original marriage contract more or less endured a decade of separations, accusations of adultery, and hasty post-nuptial agreements. Even so, with Adams inaugurated, war with France was at hand.

Jay's treaty was a betrayal in the eyes of the French. The fact that England was a sort of common-law wife to the United States was not entirely objectionable, but a *legal* union of two such infamous divorcées was intolerable. Washington had sent Charles C. Pinckney as minister to France. The government of the moment refused to receive him. Worse, that government declared any American seaman found aboard a British ship was to be treated as a pirate. The British party in the United States was now howling for French blood—led by Hamilton, who had, for his victory over the moonshiners, somehow become a major general. Dressed as such, he tried to rally the nation for war.

Adams's intention was to keep the peace, if possible, while preparing for a war that his country was in no position to fight. The French foreign minister, Talleyrand, had spent some time in exile in the United States (1793–94) and knew quite well some of the American players. In general, he dismissed the Greatest

Generation of Americans as "a nation of Debaters"; yet he was not in the least ironic when he urged Europeans to read *The Federalist*, which he thought the finest political document of the age. In later life, when asked to name the three greatest men of his time, he chose Napoleon (for so long his emperor), Pitt the Younger, and Alexander Hamilton. When Aaron Burr, in exile, called on the great minister in Paris, he was turned away with the information that His Excellency, Talleyrand, had a painting of Hamilton in his drawing room.

Happily, Talleyrand was not yet a Napoleonic duke (nor Napoleon an emperor) when he was foreign minister in 1797 to the Directory, as the government *du jour* was known. He reflected his government's fluctuating policies ever dependent on General Bonaparte's victories in the field and subversions at home. Talleyrand decided to receive the American minister for his usual fee. Talleyrand was notorious for taking bribes. But then he was endlessly practical. He liked to lecture the young foreign office clerks on the necessity of masturbating *before* coming to work, thus ensuring unclouded minds at least throughout the morning.

Adams called a special session of Congress April 14, 1797. In response to various signals from Paris, Pinckney would now be received by the Directory; in addition, Adams immediately dispatched two new ministers or commissioners to negotiate with Talleyrand: Elbridge Gerry and, fatefully, John Marshall of Virginia, destined to be a principal inventor of the nation.

John Marshall was one of fifteen children. Through his mother's family he was a Randolph and so was third cousin once removed to Thomas Jefferson, a connection not known to have given either man any pleasure, even though they shared a degree of physical likeness: each was tall, and shambling—only Marshall was dark and Jefferson carroty hued. Each was a lawyer, but where law for Jefferson was a means of knowing and assessing the world, for Marshall it proved to be a lucrative profession. Marshall's father was a lifelong friend of both George Washington and Lord Fairfax, the token neighborhood peer and great landowner.

Marshall had a good Revolution, as they say. He wintered at Valley Forge. Marshall seems to have been a born Tory. Washington was also so inclined, but both men got an education that winter when Marshall, a deputy judge advocate, in due course read the correspondence between the commanding general and the eerily corrupt Continental Congress at Philadelphia. Washington's wartime temper was an awesome volcanic affair in serial eruption when dealing with a crooked Congress that was allowing food and supplies to be sold to the British army while embezzling for themselves money appropriated for "the naked and distressed soldiers," as Washington referred to his troops. If, as was said, not quite accurately, during the Second World War that there were no atheists in foxholes, of the men at Valley Forge there could not have been many admirers of representative government. Marshall, at twenty-two, was fortunately not only physically strong but of a droll disposition; he could improvise bits of comedy with a tattered pair of silk stockings as a basis for a uniform that could never be completed. But then three thousand men could not fight at all because they had no clothes; many froze to death. Then, by June, the army was suffering from Jersey heat. The battle of Monmouth ended in confusion with a historical tableau as yet uncelebrated in the visual arts. One night Washington, Lafayette, Hamilton, Burr, Mad Anthony Wayne, and Captain-Lieutenant John Marshall all slept beneath a starry sky, slapping mosquitoes. Who won at Monmouth? No one seems to have asked. But the British left the field first.

The war concluded. The capital of Virginia moved from Williamsburg to the new town of Richmond, and John Marshall was elected to the state legislature. After a year as a delegate, Marshall, a graduate cum laude of Valley Forge, viewed the legislature with almost the same disgust as he had the infamous Continental Congress. "This long session," he wrote, "has not produced a single bill of Public importance." Plainly, he was not enamored of the people as being, collectively, God's voice. Yet at this point he could not be said to have had a political philosophy like that of Jefferson or Hamilton, or even the stern principles of the unbookish Washington. Late in life, Marshall wrote, "When I recollect the wild and enthusiastic notions with which my political opinions of that day were tinctured, I am disposed to ascribe my devotion to the Union, and to a government competent to its preservation, at least as much to casual circumstances as to judgment. 'United we stand, divided we fall' was the maxim of every orthodox American." Not a clue here to the mind and character that gave our nation *Marbury v. Madison*, planting the seed that would, over time, grow into that many-rooted ever-proliferating banyan tree which placed the Supreme Court that Gouverneur Morris had had such difficulty in thinking up things for it to do as the ultimate all-pervasive power in the republic.

By 1786 Marshall was, in effect, head of the bar at Richmond. Earlier it was Shays's rebellion that had suddenly politicized the successful young lawyer:

> These violent, I fear bloody dissentions in a state I had thought inferior in wisdom and virtue to no one in the union, added to the strong tendency which the politics of many eminent characters among ourselves have to promote private and public dishonesty, cast a deep shade over the bright prospect which the revolution of America and the establishment of our free government had opened to the votaries of liberty throughout the globe. I fear, and there is no opinion more degrading to the dignity of man, that those have truth on their side who say that man is incapable of governing himself.

Once this conviction is held, the solution that force alone is the basis of all law, a sentiment held by that most civilized of jurists Oliver Wendell Holmes Jr., becomes inevitable.

As a lawyer, Marshall specialized in property cases, starting with Lord Fairfax's five million–acre estate between the Potomac and Rappahannock rivers, the gift of a Stuart king. The land was sequestered during the Revolution. In 1787 Fairfax hired Marshall, among others, to regain his title to much of the property. Curiously, Marshall, as a working lawyer, was involved in less than a half-dozen criminal cases. Arguably, from his time as chief justice, except for the interregnum of the Warren Court, the Supreme Court has had a marked predilection for property over civil rights.

When it came time for Virginia to ratify in convention the Constitution, Marshall took what was now the strong Federalist view against such antis as Patrick Henry and George Mason. Ironically, Madison, the future Republican leader and fourth president, had put Marshall forward in the debate to defend the Constitution, specifically in the matter of the judiciary, where Henry and Mason were direly predicting "one consolidated government" that would end in tyranny. Marshall wondered just how the federal courts could do this when there were so few areas in which they would not be intruding on the prerogatives of the States. "Can they go beyond the delegated powers?" he asked. "If they were to make a law not warranted by any of the powers . . . the judges . . . would declare it void." Finally, "To what quarter will you look for protection from an infringement of the Constitution, if you will not give the power to the judiciary? There is no other body which can afford such a protection."

Marshall carried the convention: Virginia ratified the Constitution by eighty-nine votes to seventy-nine. Madison sent word to Hamilton in New York: the essential states were now united.

On May 31, 1797, President Adams selected Marshall to join Charles Pinckney and Elbridge Gerry as envoys to the French Directory. General Washington, who had liked and admired his old friend's son, received John Marshall at Mount Vernon.

A year earlier Washington had wanted to replace as minister the somewhat dim Francophile James Monroe with Marshall. But the opportunity did not arise. Now the General's successor, taking advantage of Talleyrand's apparent change of heart, had made the appointments. The visit was pleasant. The former general and his former lieutenant-captain had much in common. Marshall even reported on a new threshing machine, which the General, who had a Rube Goldberg side to him, promptly ordered. Neither man was at all literary and each must have found the company of Jefferson and Madison something of a trial. Just before Marshall's arrival, Washington noted, "I have not looked into a book since I came home, nor shall I be able to until I have discharged my workmen; probably not before the nights grow longer when possibly I may be looking into domesday book." Did they discuss the possibility of Marshall's writing the biography of Washington to the eventual horror of Jefferson? That would have been a scene.

Saturday, July 1, at Philadelphia, Minister-designate Marshall dined with President Adams. They got on well and Marshall, quite aware that Adams was the nation's senior diplomat, remained in town for three weeks learning all that he could from the old man, who was in Nestorian mood. He also saw Hamilton, who predicted, accurately, that France would soon undergo a dictatorship.

The three relatively innocent American ministers were received by Talleyrand, the perennial foreign minister. The proto-dictatorship was headed by the chief of the Directory, Barras, with the support of General Bonaparte and his all-conquering army. Talleyrand was politely indifferent to the diplomats from the New World. But one of his aides was to the point. If there was to be a treaty between the two countries, Talleyrand wanted $250,000 up front, rather like a twenty-first-century Afghan warlord. This sum would be virtuously divided among the members of the Directory. Marshall favored a prompt rejection, and a return home; his two colleagues were more cautious.

Three members of the Foreign Office, known eventually to the American public as *X*, *Y*, and *Z*, tried to extort bribes from the American ministers, who, to be precise, thought the price a bit high for what was billed as a preliminary chat. Talleyrand's office suggested that the $250,000 he expected was quite modest considering that not only had Bonaparte defeated Austria in the field but England would be next to fall and, thanks to the various links between mother country and former colonies (not least Jay's infamous treaty), the United States would be gathered up in the conquest. It was Pinckney who allegedly roared, "No, not a sixpence!" When news of the ministers' defiance got back to the States, a great cry went up: "Millions for defense but not a cent for tribute!" Hamilton led the Federalist war party, and a nation with no army to speak of and no navy was about to take on the greatest general that Europe had produced in centuries.

Meanwhile, Marshall was being wooed by a former client, Beaumarchais, author of *The Barber of Seville* and *The Marriage of Figaro*. In 1776 Beaumarchais had been the agent through whom French war supplies were sent to the United States. He had not been paid what was owed him and had retained Marshall as his lawyer. As of 1796 the suit was still pending. Talleyrand's office suggested that should Marshall win the suit for Beaumarchais, the fee could be used to sweeten the temper of the great minister. Nothing came of this, but on December 10 Marshall did get to see Napoleon Bonaparte at a reception where, among the vivid uniforms on display, he alone was simply dressed in a gray riding coat. Marshall was impressed; he also noted that Napoleon kept his hand firmly upon Talleyrand's arm. As for the threatened invasion of England, Marshall thought this sheer bluff. England controlled the seas, as every American sadly knew; and that was that.

Marshall was fifty-three days at sea on the return to New York after the interestingly but thoroughly failed mission. He was overnight a hero to the entire nation. Adams reported to

Congress the mission's failure. Adams also did his best to cool public opinion. Unfortunately, the Federalist majorities in the House and Senate had now gone collectively mad. They voted for a standing army. They created a new cabinet post, the Department of the Navy, and ordered twelve new frigates. Adams was to be known ever after, incongruously, as the Father of the American Navy.

John Adams was now presiding over a nation that liked to think itself at war with France; fortunately, the virtual dictator of France and master of much of Europe had no particular interest in the United States, or, indeed the Western Hemisphere. But in the United States, dying political parties often make colorful departures. With General Hamilton at the head of the Federalist Party, not to mention, in effect, the master of Adams's cabinet since the chief of state more and more preferred the rustic pleasures of Quincy to the intrigues—and yellow fever—of Philadelphia. When Congress rose in the spring of 1798, the presidential family, all suffering from diarrhea, fled to Quincy.

In France, power was openly shifting to General Bonaparte, who had forced the Austrian emperor to cede France the west bank of the Rhine as well as Belgium. England was now without a land buffer to the southeast. Spain was making trouble along the American southern border. Seventeen ninety-eight had begun badly for the United States; and proceeded to get worse.

At Mount Vernon, Washington was following, if not precisely leading, events. Marshall's long memorandum to Talleyrand was published in January, further adding to his national reputation and very much to the delight of General Washington, still apparently on the lookout for a surrogate son. Adams offered Marshall a seat on the Supreme Court. For a relatively young man who had gazed upon Napoleon Bonaparte, now conquering Europe, a seat on the judicial bench seemed like some sort of premature retirement from the world. It was Washington who gave Marshall his marching orders: since he was the only Federalist who could carry the Richmond district, he must be elected to the Sixth Congress from Virginia, where he became, immediately, the South's chief Federalist as of 1799.

But first, 1798 had to be got through. The long threatened war with France seemed to be off to a good start. In May a forty-four-gun frigate, *The United States*, was launched. The House then empowered all U.S. war vessels to seize any French cruisers and privateers found in American waters. Unfortunately, no one of any standing wanted to be secretary of the navy; finally, a Marylander said he would, briefly, make the financial sacrifice. Adams's call for twenty-four thousand troops got him only ten thousand, hardly enough to invade France, where Elbridge Gerry was still "negotiating" with Talleyrand. But then Gerry, as Abigail observed, always had a "wrong kink in his head." Adams was now coming to the conclusion that only a declaration of war and all that that would set in train could galvanize the United States against an enemy that every day grew more powerful. But, wisely, he hesitated. In any case, while Gerry was in Paris, Adams could not declare war.

On June 18 Marshall arrived in Philadelphia from New York. He must have looked to the political part of the nation as the next Federalist president. But Adams embraced him not as a rival but as an ally. War with France? Marshall said no. France had too many other projects afoot. If the French could not bully the United States, they would seek normal relations. Adams decided not to ask for a declaration of war, doubtless taking some joy in the fact that the absence of a war would put an end to Major General Hamilton's dream of becoming the Bonaparte of the west. Vice President Jefferson paid a call on Marshall, who was not at home. Jefferson's proto-Freudian slip has considerable charm. He left a message: "I was lucky enough not to find you at home." The "un" seems to have been forever buried in that intricate brain.

Washington wrote Adams to congratulate him on how coolly he had handled the French business; and invited John and Abigail to Mount Vernon. Adams pleaded too much work in hand. But "I must ask you sometimes for advice. We must have your name. There will be more efficacy in that than in many an army."

Since Adams was poignantly aware that his cabinet was at Hamilton's service and that Hamilton wanted to be acting commander in chief for the French war, Adams ignored his cabinet and proclaimed, ex cathedra, that he was nominating George Washington as lieutenant general and commander in chief of all the armies raised or to be raised in the United States. He got a swift confirmation from the Senate and then sent Secretary of War James McHenry to Mount Vernon.

Pickering lobbied for Hamilton as second in command. Washington said that Hamilton should be brought aboard "at almost any price." The "almost" was an alarm bell for the Hamiltonians, who had conferred with McHenry the day before he left Philadelphia.

Washington accepted the commission. McHenry took credit for persuading the General to take Hamilton as second in command.

On June 18 of our national annus horribilis, as British majesty would put it, Congress, fearful of so many alien French and Irish in our midst, extended the residence period prior to obtaining citizenship to fourteen years. The Alien Act empowered the president in wartime to seize, secure, or remove from the country all resident aliens who were citizens of the enemy nation. Since the main targets of the Federalist majority in Congress were the Republican Irish and English aliens, nothing much could be done about them unless we were actually at war.

James Lloyd, a Maryland senator, filled in the gaps with a treason and sedition bill. There would be a penalty of not more than $5,000 and imprisonment for not more than five years for any persons, aliens or citizens, who should undertake to oppose or defeat the operation of any law of the United States "or shall threaten any officer of the United States Government with any danger to his character, person or property, or attempt to procure any insurrection plot, or unlawful assembly or unlawful combination." The Sedition Act was passed on July 14, Bastille Day. The senator, aware that the First Amendment still survived his onslaught, declared that anyone could be prosecuted for "printing, writing, or speaking in a scandalous or malicious way against the government of the United States, either House in Congress, or the President, with the purpose of bringing them into contempt, stirring up sedition, or aiding and abetting a foreign nation in hostile designs against the United States." At this point, the House insisted that due process of law would still be observed and that truth was admissible in defense, unlike current legislation of a similar nature proposed and notoriously made law in our time.

Is it simply coincidence that Adams, after years of relative obscurity in the shadowy corridors of the American pantheon, has, of late, been found to be a figure of great character and intellectual interest as, indeed, he was and is? But one wonders whether those who would now place him on high might indeed be otherwise enthralled by the fact that, ignoring the Bill of Rights, he approved the Alien-Sedition Acts not only in time of war but even in the face of a dangerous possibility of . . . well, danger, some time or other in days to come.

Predictably, Republicans howled. The First Amendment had been struck down. They howled even louder when a judge ordered the arrest of Benjamin Franklin Bache, a grandson of the wise man and an editor of a Republican paper, on the ground that he had libeled the president by suggesting that the correspondence of Elbridge Gerry, submitted to Congress, had been forged. Adams, who had always hated Bache and his lies—or "lies," as the case may be—was delighted. He even used the oldest line of tyrants: things are worse over there. Had Bache been a *French* editor, he would have been guillotined.

Apologists for the Federalists are once again being heard in the land. After all, in 1798 the republic was less than ten years old, while all of thirty thousand Frenchmen, possibly up to no good, were abroad in our alabaster cities. Page Smith (*John Adams*, Doubleday, 1962), an admirably thorough court biographer, writes that "according to Jefferson. . . the mere threat of the Alien bill so alarmed the numerous French agents in the country that . . . they chartered a ship to carry as many of them as could crowd aboard back to France." Mr. Smith gives no source. In any case, he believes, "We can leave the Alien and Sedition Acts to the periodic indignation of righteous historians who will be happy if their own nation and their own times show no grosser offenses against human freedom." He notes that "Jefferson, of course [of course!], viewed the Alien and Sedition Acts as the first step toward tyranny, as 'merely an experiment on the American mind to see how far it will bear an avowed violation of the constitution.'" In history, a first step tends to encourage a second until as *King Lear* puts it: "The weight of this sad time we must obey, speak what we feel; not what we ought to say."

If ever there was a time when Benjamin Franklin's fear for John Adams was fulfilled, 1798 was the year when he was "out of his senses." He made no effort to soften the Alien and Sedition Acts. In fact, comfortable with his new powers to decide under the Alien Act whom he might deport, he wrote Pickering about one Victor du Pont de Nemours, son of a friend of Jefferson, "I shall not be so guilty of so much affection or regard to science, as to be very willing to grant passports to du Pont de Nemours, or any other French philosophers, in the present situation of our Country. We had had too many French philosophers already." While still apparently out of his senses, Adams insisted that his feckless and somewhat shady son-in-law, William Stephens Smith, be appointed adjutant general to Washington. Pickering vowed to kill the appointment, while McHenry got Washington to oppose it. The Senate simply struck out Smith's name.

General Washington, again commander in chief of American forces, sent his nephew Bushrod Washington to collect John Marshall and deliver him to Mount Vernon. Marshall, having turned down the Supreme Court, hardly wanted to go to Congress. Washington said it was his sacred duty. Marshall said, "I had made large pecuniary engagements which required close attention to my profession."

Washington pulled rank. He had spent the prime of his life— sixteen years—in the service of his country and now in his old age and bad health was again on duty. The least that the youthful

Marshall could do . . . Marshall later reported, "My resolution yielded to this representation."

Meanwhile, Marshall's campaign for Congress was not easy. The Alien and Sedition Acts inflamed Jefferson's potentially majority party and disaffected a number of Federalists, including Marshall, who said, tactlessly, that had he been in Congress he would have voted against them. It was a stormy October all round. Fortunately, Adams regained his senses. With an American naval success or two against the French, Talleyrand was beginning to question the value of any war against this new maritime power.

The new navy was a success. But, thanks to Hamilton, the army was in a state of confusion. Hamilton insisted on being second in command to Washington, which would have made him, in effect, the actual commander. But Henry Knox outranked Hamilton from Revolutionary days, and he refused to serve under Hamilton. Adams took Knox's side. McHenry said that the ranking came straight from Washington, not mentioning that he himself had brought letters from Hamilton and Pickering in order to influence the General.

Adams now laid down the law: I am the president. It is my responsibility as commander in chief to decide. Although, in theory, Adams said he was willing to resign as president in favor of Washington (constitutionally an impossibility), he had no intention of allowing Washington to perform the presidential office while Adams occupied it. Then the nightmare of John Adams's political life broke over a head now possessed of its senses. The General, like some ancient lion who had lost none of its territorial sense, struck.

On September 21 Washington wrote McHenry: "I can perceive pretty clearly that the matter is, or very soon will be, brought to the alternative of submitting to the President's forgetfulness of what I considered a compact or a condition of acceptance of the appointment . . . or to return him my commission. You will recollect, too that, my acceptance being conditional, I requested you to take the commission back that it might be restored or annulled according to the President's determination to accept or reject the terms on which I had offered to serve."

Before Adams could respond to McHenry, the General wrote him what a later time would call a Dear John letter. Washington may not have been much of a field general, but he was a master of human strategy. He struck Adams at his weakest point: the appointment of his feckless son-in-law as Washington's adjutant general. This was not only lèse-majesté but it violated their original agreement. As for Hamilton, Washington made it clear that his loss would be "irreparable."

Adams wisely collapsed before this display of force majeure. Hamilton would be number two; Washington would select his own adjutant general. But Adams was not exactly defeated. He observed to Washington how expensive it was to maintain an army with no war. "At present there is no more prospect of seeing a French army here than in Heaven." Adams sent the Senate

Washington's acceptance of the commission. The nation was delighted even as the war spirit lessened outside high Federalist circles. In Paris, du Pont de Nemours, doubtless well-briefed by Jefferson, explained to Talleyrand that the American mood had hardened against France's repeated insults. Talleyrand advised the Directory that the game of bluff and bribes seemed to have been played out. Jefferson, his eye on the election of 1800, not only was constitutionally committed to peace, he realized that a Federalist war against France, no matter how ill-conducted by Hamilton and friends, would hardly—win or lose—be in the Republican interest. In only thirteen months there would be an election in which the party of the true people must prevail. It is likely that as of August 1798, when the country was distressed by the news that Washington had been struck by the ague and had lost twenty pounds, Adams was thinking along not dissimilar lines.

By mid-September, Washington was on the mend; but Philadelphia had been struck by yellow fever, and, in Quincy, Abigail was seriously ill. Adams wrote: "The last has been the most gloomy summer of my life, and the prospect of a winter is more dismal still." He seems to have toyed, not seriously, with the thought of resignation, particularly when contemplating the return to Philadelphia for the opening of Congress because the alternative would be to "give up." He began to prepare his message to Congress. He canvassed the cabinet: "Whether it will be expedient for the President to recommend . . . a declaration of war against France?" If not, whom should he send to restore diplomatic relations? Patrick Henry, say?

The Hamiltonian cabinet was dismayed at this change in mood. Hamilton got Treasury Secretary Wolcott to draft a letter to the effect that a declaration of war was inexpedient, as was sending yet another minister, which "would be an act of humiliation." For party purposes, a nation readying itself for war was preferable to one actually at war with Bonaparte, who had the dismaying habit of defeating those who opposed him. Finally, the career of Hamilton still depended, as it had from the beginning of his ascent, on the necessity of war as a shortcut for the classic hero to rise once again. Washington and Hamilton, side by side, as they had been at the dawn of the Republic's history. Adams would have no chance against two such paladins.

In November, Adams set out for Philadelphia. Abscessed teeth gave him great pain. Abigail's absence in Quincy was not calculated to improve his mood as he prepared for the great battle of his presidency. "Children, you know," he wrote Abigail, "when they are toothing, are somewhat fretful, and the toothing of the second childhood is equally apt to make peevish. But though my mouth is so sore as to give me a sore throat and an headache, I am neither fretful nor peevish." Adams was now pulling himself together. Was the world wide enough for him and Hamilton?

He might have echoed Burr had Burr expressed himself on this delicate subject so early. He also drew strength from a text of Edmund Burke: "Power and eminence and consideration are things not to be begged. They must be commanded and they who supplicate mercy from others can never hope for justice through themselves. Often has a man lost his all because he wouldn't submit to hazard all in defending it."

Adams spoke in a temperate mood to Congress. Jefferson suspected, in the matter of France, some sinister intrigue. But what? The president's New Year's 1799 reception for officialdom was made festive not only by numerous new military officers who helped drink thirty gallons of punch but by Lord Nelson's victory over the French at the Nile. The British fleet had made a comeback in the Mediterranean. "The English," remarked Adams, "have exhibited an amazing example of skill and intrepidity. We are a chip off that block."

Meanwhile, the ongoing debate in Congress over the Alien and Sedition Acts was suddenly complicated by the "secret" intervention of Vice President Jefferson. Deeply alarmed by the Federal assault on the Bill of Rights, not to mention "the Federalist reliance on grand juries . . . to be inquisitors on the freedom of speech, writing and of principle of their fellow citizens," Jefferson and Madison went underground. Jefferson was president of that Senate which had passed the Sedition Act of which he so totally disapproved. At home in Virginia, Madison was also trying to overthrow what each man regarded not only as two dangerously unconstitutional measures but, more specifically, a direct attack by the Federalists upon the Republican Party and its greatest weapon, the Republican-edited press. Of the two, Jefferson's situation was the most delicate, since he was heavily associated in the public mind with the unloved French party. Also, as vice president of the United States, he had sworn to uphold a protean constitution which he wished to save from the Alien and Sedition Acts, now the laws of the land. It was also clear to him that according to the language of the Sedition Act, he himself could be charged by a Federalist court with sedition.

What Jefferson and Madison actually did is somewhat occluded to this day. There is little correspondence between the two men during this period for fear of postal surveillance; Jefferson complained: "I know not what mortifies me more, that I should fear to write what I think, or my country bear such a state of things." It is clear, though, that they took the position that the Sedition Act was designed to eliminate the First Amendment. Since John Marshall's great invention of judicial review was not yet custom, much less law, Jefferson looked about for some other power that could override Congress and president: a referendum of the people at large (direct democracy for which none of the inventors was prepared)? Rather, to turn to the constituent States themselves. The Tenth Amendment had reserved to them "or to the people" those powers not delegated to the United States. Plainly, before Federalist judges began an all-out arrest of political enemies, the States, through their legislatures, must denounce the two acts and make them void. The combined ingenuity of Madison, the essential inventor of the Constitution, and Jefferson, the voice of the people's independence from tyrannous government, was considerable. But on every side there was great danger.

The two men made their case against the actions of the federal government in the form of resolutions to be sent to the state legislatures in the hope that each would ratify the resolution, thus declaring the two acts unconstitutional and not law. As much as possible the minatory word *nullification* was got around. To accept the principle that any state could nullify any act of the national government was, plainly, disunion, and disunion was no nation, and no nation was unthinkable to two statesmen so committed to what Jefferson thought of as "the empire of liberty." But Congress, for party reasons, had overthrown freedom of speech, due process of law, and who knew what range of other ancillary and basic rights thus far taken for granted.

In all of this, Adams and Hamilton are not in the forefront. Adams would need Republican votes if he was to be reelected, while Hamilton's brilliant lawyerly mind had, in two Federalist papers, anticipated the Jefferson-Madison dilemma. From Federalist No. 26: "The State legislatures who will always be not only vigilant but suspicious and jealous guardians of the rights of the citizens against encroachments from the federal government, will constantly have their attention awake to the conduct of the national government, and will be ready enough, if anything improper appears, to sound the alarm to the people, and not only to be the voice, but if necessary the ARM of discontent." It is possible that Jefferson had not read this, but Madison, coauthor of *The Federalist*, would have known it well and could easily have deeply embarrassed the aborning Bonaparte. But Hamilton was not brought into the matter.

Jefferson's authorship of the Kentucky Resolutions became known only some years after his retirement, while Madison's authorship of the Virginia Resolutions was not known until he had been safely elected president. The two resolutions boiled down to states' rights versus those of the central government. Neither resolution made much of a contemporary mark. (The North ignored the invitation to adopt similar resolutions, and in due course the Acts expired with the Adams administration in 1801.) Where Jefferson and Madison saw the legislatures of the States as bulwark for the protection of the people's rights, John Marshall's 1803 decision in *Marbury v. Madison* provided the working machinery in the form of "judicial review" by the Supreme Court to undo "errors" of the legislative or executive branches. Errors of the judiciary can be rectified only by impeachment—which President Jefferson tried, unsuccessfully, to do in the case of a particularly rabid Federalist justice, Samuel Chase.

As a member of the Virginia legislature, Madison got the resolution (in language milder than Jefferson's Kentucky Resolution) adopted in the form of a condemnation of the Alien and Sedition Acts as "palpable and alarming infractions of the Constitution."

The vice president, back on his senatorial throne in Philadelphia, left to his ally John Breckinridge the task of steering the resolution through the Kentucky legislature. In the end, the essential arguments still obtain to this day. Particularly, to *this* day, in much the language of Jefferson and Madison, but the revolutionary issue of a state's right to nullify a federal law awaits some centrifugal catastrophe before enactment.

Although it is safe to assume that Jefferson never changed his mind about the great threat the Alien and Sedition Acts posed to a free people, Adams in old age renewed their friendship.

On June 14, 1813, while their friend Madison, now president, was fleeing the British as they burned down the unfinished city of Washington, Adams wrote Jefferson,

> In your letter to Dr. Priestley of March 21, 1801, you . . .
> disclaim the legitimacy of that libel on legislation. This
> Law, I presume was, the Alien law.
>
> As your name is subscribed to that law, as Vice President, and mine as President, I know not why you are not as responsible for it as I am. [*Tu quoque* is the best defense.] Neither of Us were concerned in the formation of it. We were then at War with France. [Not really, thanks to Adams.] French spies then swarmed in our cities and in the Country. Some of them were intolerably, turbulent, impudent and seditious. To check these was the design of this law. Was there ever a Government which had not Author-

ity to defend itself against Spies in its own Bosom? Spies
of an Ennemy at War? This law was never executed by me,
in any Instance.

But what is the conduct of our Government now? Aliens
are ordered to report their names and obtain Certificates
once a month: and an industrious Scotchman at this moment industriously labouring in my Garden is obliged to
walk once a month to Boston, eight miles at least, to renew
his Certificate from the Marshall. And a fat organist is ordered into the Country, etc., etc., etc. . . . all this is right.
Every government has by the Law of Nations a right to
make prisoners of War, of every Subject of an Enemy. But
a War with England differs not from a War with France.
The Law of Nations is the same on both.

In a sense Jefferson had made his case in the first Kentucky
Resolution from which Breckinridge had eliminated the core argument "where powers are assumed [by the Federal government]
which have not been delegated [in the Constitution], a nullification of the act is the rightful remedy: that every State has a natural right in cases not within the compact . . . to nullify of their
own authority all assumptions of powers by others within their
own limits." Thus Jefferson in 1798 had spoken in favor of the
principle of nullification. But the first resolution asked for no
more than a general sense of the States that the two Federalist
Acts were unconstitutional. The man who had once—rashly?—

said that "the tree of liberty must be refreshed from time to time with the blood of patriots and tyrants" was indeed on record that if a state denied liberty to its lawful citizens, revolution is, as it was in 1776, the weapon of choice. This is a great truth savagely if not fatally tested by a Civil War in which the abolition of slavery replaced disunion, despite Lincoln's most poetic efforts to the contrary, and any hope of a decentralized Union as the issue has been dead until this day.

Seven

By February 1799 Talleyrand realized that his American policy was metastasizing into a mess. With vast effort (and expense) the military genius of the age could conquer the United States, but to what end? French Louisiana contained almost as much territory as the United States and was only a source of vexation, while France's ongoing war with England needed a new element. Why not make an ally of the United States or at least play the two enemies off against each other? His Excellency let it be known to the American president that he would be happy to receive an American minister at Paris on the terms proposed by Mr. Adams. Adams immediately saw his opportunity to be known not only as a peacemaker loved by the Lord but as the joyous executioner of Hamilton's war policy, not to mention political career. Also, no more irritable notes about precedence from the now totally retired General at Mount Vernon.

Adams announced the resumption of diplomatic relations with the United States' oldest ally. He did this without consulting his cabinet, to a man in thrall to Hamilton. He ordered two envoys to leave from Trenton; then he returned to Quincy. Arguably, his persistent residence there was his political downfall. In Adams's absence, Hamilton worked on the cabinet to delay the departure of the new envoys. Not until October, back in Philadelphia, did Adams realize how he had been undercut. He personally ordered the diplomatic mission to depart. He was also out for blood. He had a little list. Secretary of State Pickering was at the top, followed by Wolcott at Treasury and McHenry at War.

Once the president was back at the seat of government, Hamilton was entirely boxed in since the sources of his actual power were his influence over Adams's cabinet and, of course, the fact that he was inspector general of the army commanded by General Washington, enjoying ill health at Mount Vernon.

Adams had a stormy scene with McHenry, who dared voice his objection to the French mission. On May 31, McHenry, in a state of shock at the president's rage, wrote a memorandum for Adams confirming his resignation. This is the only "character scene," in dialogue, that we have of Adams in action.

War Department, May 31, 1800

I respectfully take the Liberty to state to you my recollection of the substance and incidents of the conversation which passed between us on the evening (the 5th instant) preceding my Resignation of the Office of Secretary for the Department of War . . .

P[resident] Hamilton is an intriguant—the greatest intriguant in the world—a man devoid of every moral principle—a Bastard—and as much a foreigner as Gallatin. Mr. Jefferson is an infinitely better man; a wiser one I am sure, and, if President, will act wisely. I know it and would rather be vice president under him, or even minister resident at the Hague, than indebted to such a being as Hamilton for the presidency. But I can retire to Quincy, and like Washington write letters, and leave them behind me. You are subservient to Hamilton, who ruled Washington and would still rule if he could. Washington saddled me with three secretaries who would controul me; but I shall take care of that. Wolcott is a good Secretary of the Treasury, but what do any of you know of the diplomatic interests of Europe? You are all mere children who can give no assistance in such matters.

S[ecretary] I am very ready to acknowledge your superior opportunities and experience in Affairs of Diplomacy, and, if you please my own comparative ignorance.

P How could such men dictate to me in such matters or dare to recommend a suspension of the Mission to France? . . . You cannot, Sir, remain longer in office.

On May 10 Adams asked for Pickering's resignation. Pickering countered, somewhat originally, with the observation that he needed the salary. Wolcott, allegedly the most Hamiltonian of the lot, remained on until the end of the year. Adams then offered the War Department to Marshall, who turned it down; next he offered him the State Department, which, after two weeks of meditation, he accepted. Marshall's popularity in the Federalist Party soothed many of Hamilton's partisans.

❧

George Washington apparently still retained a degree of confidence in the three secretaries he had "saddled" Adams with. In October, Washington wrote Hamilton about the president's late decision: "I was surprised at the *measure*, how much more so at the manner of it? This business [the mission to France] seems to have commenced in an evil hour, and under unfavorable auspices; and I wish mischief may not tread in all its steps, and be the final result." It is difficult to tell exactly where Washington stood in the French matter. From experience he did not trust Talleyrand; yet in his Farewell Address he was not eager to promote wars with great European powers. From Washington's tactful letters it is hard to determine to what extent General Hamilton had brought him into the war party whose only beneficiary would be Hamilton. Should the financial wizard defeat Bonaparte in the field somewhere, somehow, a most unlikely prospect for the highly literate, not to mention numerate, Lord Keynes of his day, to do.

But the suicidal tendencies of the Federalist Party were no longer for Washington to deal with. In the autumnal light of his last days, the shadow of Jefferson was now clearly visible across their common Virginia land and well into the nation beyond as the voting began in November.

On November 17, riding back from church, Washington fell heavily to the ground. Quickly he was on his feet; and remounted. Earlier in this day, he had written a response to a long letter in which McHenry had described his scene with Adams . . . "with the contents of which," Washington wrote, "I have been stricken dumb." Apropos the split between president and cabinet, Washington wrote, "They appear to me to be moving by hasty strides to some awful crisis." One awful crisis was Pennsylvania voting Republican, securing that state for Jefferson and Burr. McHenry appeared to be fishing for a statement from Washington who, far too clever to join in a battle not of his choosing, wrote, "I believe that it is better that I should remain mute than express any sentiments on the important matters which are related." Then he let go the scepter for good: "The vessel is afloat, or very nearly so, and myself, as a passenger only, I shall trust to the mariners whose duty it is to watch, to steer it into a safe port."

On December 10 the Potomac Company met in Alexandria: Washington did not attend but sent his proxy vote.

The night of December 11, Washington looked out the window and saw a great circle around the moon. A dramatic change in the weather was due.

The morning of December 12, he answered a letter from Hamilton about the advisability of starting a military academy to train American officers. Recalling, perhaps, problems created by the Order of the Cincinnati, he left this matter to the new secretary of war. This proved to be Washington's last letter, and the weather had indeed changed dramatically that day: hail, snow, rain, increasing cold; yet for five hours he made the round of his farms.

When he got home, a servant noted that there were flecks of snow in his hair. He franked some letters but said that the weather was too bad to send a servant to the post office that evening. Then he went straight in to dinner, not changing first into dry clothes.

On Friday morning, December 13, the fields were white with snow, which was still falling. Despite a sore throat, Washington went out for a walk before sunset. A northeast wind. After the evening meal, in spite of a worsening hoarse voice, he read aloud to Martha items from the various gazettes and newspapers. The Republican James Monroe had just won the governorship of Virginia, and a Republican sweep was indicated for the state. When it was suggested that Washington take medicine for his throat, he remarked that he never took anything for something so "trifling." Of the cold, he said, "Let it go as it came."

Between 2 and 3 o'clock the next morning he woke Martha to tell her he was ill. He could barely speak. The ague: fever and chills, often chronic, often malarial in origin. Battle of Mon-

mouth? Washington would not allow Martha to go for help—
she had just recovered from a serious illness. At 7:00 a servant
came to light the fire. A doctor was sent for. Washington was
having trouble breathing; a palliative of molasses, vinegar, and
butter nearly suffocated him. The General insisted that he be
bled. Martha thought, rightly, that this would be worse than the
ague. But a pint of blood was taken. He was dressed, sat by the
fire. Doctors came. Washington sent for two wills. He gave them
to Martha, telling her which one to burn. In late afternoon,
Washington said to a friend, Colonel Lear, "I find I am going, my
breath cannot continue long; I believed from the first attack it
would be fatal . . . " In the presence, later, of his doctors, he repeated, "I feel myself going. I thank you for your attention. You
had better not take any more trouble about me; but let me go off
quietly; I cannot last long."

After a restless evening trying to get his breath, he said, at
10 P.M., "I am just going. Have me decently buried, and do not let
my body be put into the vault in less than two days after I am
dead." To be buried alive was a very real terror of that day. Washington looked at Lear, "Do you understand me?" Lear said, "Yes,
sir." And Washington said, "'Tis well." Lear held Washington's
hand for a time. Then the General, suddenly, removed it and
took his own pulse. The hand fell back. Lear held it to his chest
while Dr. Craik shut the blue-gray eyes which had now, finally,
gazed into the common domesday book.

Martha asked, "Is he gone?" Lear nodded. She said, as her husband had, "'Tis well. . . . All is now over. I have no more trials to pass through. I shall soon follow him."

The head of the mahogany casket was inscribed *Surge ad Judicium*. Then, on a silver plate, *General George Washington Departed this life on the 14th of December 1799, Aet. 67*.

❧ Some After Words ❧

I am at the end of the space allotted. Since I have already described the most important, not to mention ambiguous, deed of Jefferson's career, the Louisiana Purchase, I leave you with President John Adams's great-grandson Henry Adams and his nine-volume *History of the United States of America During the Administrations of Thomas Jefferson and James Madison* which was, at least for my generation, the essential—and certainly most witty—analysis of these formative years. In fact, the actual physical possession of those volumes was, for many of us, totemic. Years ago I asked the critic Elizabeth Hardwick if her divorce from poet Robert Lowell had been in any way difficult. "Oh, not at all," she said, "except, of course, the usual intellectuals' quarrel over which of us should get Henry Adams's history."

In the early seventies, when I was writing a book about Aaron Burr, I read the standard—and not so standard—texts of the day. These included Dumas Malone's multivolume life of Jefferson. In my youth, I was fascinated by dramatic contradictions in character; in age, I am far more interested in those consistencies wherein lie greatness like Washington's throughout his career, or overwrought conscience like Adams's, throughout his. First time around, Dumas Malone annoyed me with his denial that Jefferson could not have had children by his slave Sally Hemings because no gentleman would have done so in the South, and as he was the greatest gentleman of Virginia . . . On this weak syllogism, a false character was constructed.

I am now more moved by Jefferson and the Nullification Resolutions (even in Dumas Malone) where Jefferson's inner consistency about maintaining liberty within a state suddenly turned onerous comes up sharply against the problem of what to do when a heretofore virtuous republican government gets the votes in the two houses of Congress as well as that of a chief executive willing to collude with them in an assault on the Bill of Rights. Inevitably, Jefferson would think that if the States had not the right to nullify the central government's tyrannous acts, they should leave the Union.

In 1860 the South thought that as each of their states had entered the Union voluntarily each had the right, using Jefferson's own language, to secede on grounds similar to his: "When in the course of human events, it becomes necessary for one people to dissolve the political bonds which have connected them with another, and to assume, among the powers of the earth, the separate and equal station to which the laws of nature and of nature's God entitled them, a decent respect to the opinion of mankind requires that they should declare the causes which impel them to the separation." So far so good. Certainly an elimination of the First Amendment in itself would be a sufficient cause for secession or even rebellion.

But the great contradiction comes a few lines later. Jefferson lived with it uncomfortably for all his life, while the South spent four years dying with it on a hundred battlefields: "We hold these truths to be self-evident: that all men are created equal: that they are endowed by their Creator with certain inalienable rights: that among these are life, liberty, and the pursuit of happiness." But as of 1776 most African-Americans lived in slavery, and, in any case, each was counted in the Constitution itself not as a person but as a fraction of a whole person—which could only be, for purposes of citizenship, a white man. The various Indian tribes and nations were excluded from many inalienable rights, as were all women, who could not vote, or like those of us brought up in the District of Columbia (until we moved away).

The exuberantly expansionist Jeffersonian generation kept at bay the contradiction. Lincoln sidestepped the real issue—slavery—by moving the matter to what he took to be a higher plane, the integrity, the indivisibility of the Union. Secession, as a solution, was successfully put down. But what about those wrongs that neither federal nor state governments would put right? Enter John Marshall.

On December 16, 1800, soon-to-be former President Adams offered the chief justiceship to John Jay, who had once held—and relinquished—the post. The current chief justice was resigning due to ill health. Jay's response to Adams was quick. "I left the bench perfectly convinced that under a system so defective it would not obtain the energy, weight, and dignity which, as the last resort of the justice of the nation, it should possess." He said, no. Plainly actual "original intent" of the Constitution did not impress the first chief justice.

Since Republicans were not appointed federal judges during the first dozen years of the republic, the victorious Republican Party was all set to redress the balance. But Adams's term did not end until March 4. He now had three months in which to appoint Federalists to the judiciary, leaving a lasting mark on the new government. On January 2, 1801, the lame duck Federalist majority in the House passed the New Judiciary Bill, authorizing new judges. That same day, Adams, without consulting Secretary of State Marshall, sent his name to the Senate for confirmation as chief justice of the United States. A week later the unprotesting Marshall was confirmed.

On February 4, Adams began to appoint a quantity of judges and justices of the peace, U.S. marshalls, attorneys, clerks, and sixteen circuit courts, each complete with Federalist judge. By March 3, at 9:00 P.M., with Marshall's help, the job was done.

Meanwhile, Jefferson, in ecumenical mood, had written Marshall a note, "May I hope the favor of your attendance to administer the oath?"

March 4 was Jefferson's inaugural day. Adams was not a good sport: some hours before he had started on his way back to Massachusetts and so he missed the dramatic moment when the two cousins, Jefferson and Marshall, faced each other in the only completed section of the Capitol at Washington, the Senate chamber.

Arguably the great division in American political life has been between the original Federalists and Republicans (they keep changing their names, even assuming one another's identity, as circumstances and opportunity require). Their polar aspects, for those who enjoy personalizing the abstract, are Hamilton and Jefferson. Hamilton: "A national debt, if not excessive, will be to us a national blessing." Today's Hamiltonians have beatified our present nation with a debt undreamed of by Hamilton, who also took the Federalist dark view of democracy: The people is a great beast. Opposite to Hamilton is the benign Jefferson who assured us that, simply by birth, we have (his *original* words) "inalienable rights among which are the preservation of life and liberty, and the pursuit of happiness." That the actual pursuit of happiness is, in and of itself, the only true happiness that most of us will ever know might be the Puritan Adamsian gloss on what was more Jefferson's great daydream than any working political philosophy. More to the point, Jefferson versus Marshall was to be the great drama that, to this day, divides us.

Before the election, Marshall was one of the extreme Federalists who enjoyed calling the Republicans "Democrats." A very bad word indeed since it was associated with France's bloody terror in the days of the Jacobin ascendancy, now swept away by First Consul Bonaparte, soon to be Emperor-dictator of the French. The morning of March 4, Marshall started a letter to Pinckney: "The Democrats are divided into speculative theorists and absolute terrorists. With the latter I am disposed to class Mr. Jefferson." After the inauguration, he concluded his letter. "I have administered the oath to the Presd. His inauguration speech . . . well judged and conciliatory . . . is in direct terms giving the lie to the violent party declamation which has elected him, but it is strongly characteristic of the general cast of this political theory."

There was continuing Republican criticism of Adams's "midnight judges." Meanwhile, Marshall was diplomatically silent on political issues of the day. Instead Marshall began a restructuring of the Court. Henceforth, the chief justice himself would, with few exceptions, deliver the Court's opinion. Since no one in charge had thought of the Court as needing a courthouse, the Senate generously lent them a committee room on the main floor of the Capitol. (Later the Court was tactlessly moved to the basement.) In Marshall's spare time, in those happy days abundant, he was busy negotiating with the publisher of what would become his vast biography of Washington. It was during this time that the fruit, as it were, of his joint work with Adams appeared before the Supreme Court.

On March 2, forty-two men, appointed by President Adams as justices of the peace for the District of Columbia, had been confirmed by the then-Federalist Senate; Marshall, as secretary of state, had also signed their commissions. Marshall's successor at State, James Madison, came across the file and was duly annoyed. The village of Washington and the ten square miles of the District of Columbia might have accommodated two or three JPs but not forty-two. This was a patronage grab on the grand scale by a lame duck president and a dead duck political party. Madison and Jefferson agreed that twenty-six JPs were more than enough, thus eliminating sixteen. Four of the rejects petitioned the Supreme Court to issue a writ of mandamus against Secretary of State Madison to force him to commission one of the four, by name William Marbury.

Marshall issued an order to Madison, by name, to show cause why the writ should *not* be granted. On December 8 Jefferson sent his first message to Congress. (He did not personally accompany it, and for 112 years presidents did not appear in person to read their messages.) Jefferson spoke of Adams's judiciary act and said there was insufficient business to warrant such an increase in courts and judges. Jefferson had an even more significant passage in his message which, had he retained it, might have changed the course of constitutional history: each Federal government department has the right to be its own judge, according to its own "judgments and uncontrolled by the opinion of any other departments." Of the Sedition Law, he wrote, "I do declare that I hold that act to be in palpable and unqualified contradiction to the Constitution. Considering it then as a nullity, I have relieved from oppression under it those of my fellow citizens who were within reach of the functions confided to me."

This passage was struck because Jefferson feared that "the public might be made to misunderstand" that any state or government branch was its own interpreter of the Constitution. Yet he himself saw no alternative but "the tyranny of the courts." He was prematurely prescient. With hindsight, one now thinks it might have been best if the true war between the cousins had been out in the open earlier.

The Senate took up the matter first. That "elegant specimen" *(New York Post)* Gouverneur Morris himself appeared, doubtless still unaware of what an amount of work "his" Court would find to do once it had polished off the last of those Admiralty suits he regarded as their makework. But Breckinridge of Kentucky shifted the debate from any notion of judicial review to the less dangerous issue of a partisan creation of far more judges and courts than the country needed. On a party vote (Republicans sixteen, Federalists fifteen) Adams's handiwork was voted down.

The House followed the Senate. The judiciary act was dead. On September 22 Marshall signed his contract to write the *Life of Washington* in five volumes; then he went, grumbling, on circuit. Jefferson was now busy with the Louisiana Purchase.

By chance, the members of the Supreme Court occupied the same boarding house near the Capitol, and *Marbury v. Madison* continued to engage their interest. Former Attorney General Lee represented Marbury before the Court. The justices came to a quick decision: they had already heard enough about the case in the congressional debates as well as in argument before them. Was Marbury entitled to his salary and the commission that went with it? Marshall said yes: Marbury was a justice of the peace as of the Senate's ratification. Could he be withdrawn by the next president and Congress? If so, and should there be an argument over what was due to him as a matter of law, who interprets the law? The courts, said Marshall.

Question: how far could the courts go in interfering with the arrangements of the executive branch, particularly in the case of the Supreme Court, its equal? Foreign affairs, political actions were regarded as outside the Court's domain, but where a *law* had been violated . . . Marshall liked to make analogies. Should a government officer, required by law to deliver land-patents to purchasers, *not* deliver a paid-for patent, what recourse did the purchaser have? The courts. What else? With that Marshall laid the foundation for judicial review. But now, practically speaking, he and the Court were helpless. If they should order Madison to give Marbury his commission, Jefferson would not only ignore the Court, as Jackson and Lincoln were later to do, but he might then introduce his—to Marshall, certainly—revolutionary limitation of the Court's right to review the acts of the States and so on.

Marshall slipped out the back door; he acknowledged that the legitimately appointed Marbury ought to have redress but the writ of mandamus that his lawyer had demanded of Madison was, under Section 13 of the Judiciary Act of 1789, "repugnant to the Constitution," and void. The whole case must be thrown out of court as there was no applicable law violated.

Marshall was now a strict constructionist. Since the Constitution nowhere gave Congress the power to add or subtract from the Court's original jurisdiction, the 1789 act had been dead on arrival. Thus Marshall settled Jefferson's hash without the civil war which his heirs on the Court helped bring on—literally, by abstracting from *Marbury v. Madison* the principle of judicial review that then took a tragic turn when the Court declared unconstitutional (1857) the act of Congress known as the Missouri Compromise, barring slaves (like one Dred Scott) from "free" territory.

Finally, Marshall's most ingenious chimera *(Dartmouth College v. Woodward):* "A corporation is an artificial being, invisible, intangible, and existing only in contemplation of law." Marshall's adjectives are compelling since they are usually applied, in this Godly republic, to God Himself if the word *law* is replaced by *awe.* This judgment is the cornerstone of modern Toryism.

Bernard Bailyn is always a good historian to consult in these matters. In his recent *To Begin the World Anew*, he concentrates on the formative years of the republic. In a short note on *The Federalist and the Supreme Court* he also examines just how many citations from *The Federalist* papers the Court has used, from Marshall to this day. In *McCulloch v. Maryland*, Marshall rejects a defense attorney's citation from *The Federalist* with the cautionary—deflationary?—"No tribute can be paid to their worth, which exceeds their merit; but in applying their opinions to the cases which may arise in the progress of our government, a right to judge of their correctness must be retained."

For most of the nineteenth century through the 1920s, the justices referred to the sacred tablets only occasionally. The most quoted were Hamilton No. 32, on exclusive and concurrent powers of taxation, and Madison No. 42, on powers delegated to the federal government. From the 1930s through the 1980s references increased. "Why the increase in citations?" Bailyn asks, "Why the papers' increasing importance and sanctity?" Surprisingly, the so-called originalists on the Court, like Thomas and Scalia, seldom advert to them. Of the current Court, only the noble John Paul Stevens is most attentive to his predecessors. Bailyn makes the compelling case that the Court has not used—does not use—*The Federalist* as "a treatise on political theory or a masterwork on political science, but [as] a guide to the disposition of power in specific circumstances, an authority on the constitutional use of force and the constraints on the use of force in the intricate functioning of the federalist system of government in America." Oliver Wendell Holmes Jr. is smiling in limbo; William James nods agreement. Thomas Jefferson is currently negotiating a return, watering can in hand.

For those radicals who are always among us, it should be noted that we are not a nation "under God." God is mentioned only twice in *The Federalist*, each time by James Madison, a clergyman's son, who uses God as in the "only Heaven knows" sense. That is, if memory serves: in my old, now lost, copy of *The Federalist* God was mentioned twice in the index, while in the 1996 version he does not appear in the index at all. Political correctness? "Democracy" does get three references. The only useful one, as is so often the case, comes from Madison No. 10: "The two great points of difference between a democracy and a republic are: first, the delegation of the government; in the latter, to a small number of citizens elected by the rest; secondly, the greater number of citizens, and greater sphere of country over which the latter may be extended." Did he suspect that his friend Jefferson would, in a dozen years, buy Louisiana? But Madison's good sense deserts him as we, the wiser in future time, now know when he expatiates on the virtues of a large over a small republic as Montesquieu preferred. Madison opts for the large because: "it will be more difficult for unworthy candidates to practice with success the vicious arts by which elections are too often carried . . . " Well, as Joe E. Brown observed, no one is perfect. Meanwhile, let us hope that instead of a homely watering can, Jefferson Redux does not return with a guillotine.

One bright morning in 1961 at Hyannis beside the cold sea, after a vigorous game of backgammon, which I won, John F. Kennedy sat back, lit a cigar in the respite before his brother Bobby's arrival from his house within the Kennedy compound.

"Your uncle Lefty Lewis . . ." Jack began.

"Not my uncle . . ."

"But he's Jackie's uncle . . ."

"He's not her uncle either. He was married to our stepfather's sister, where he got the money to collect Walpole."

"*Merrywood!*" Jack bit his cigar at the thought of that Virginia house from which emerged Jackie and I and a thundering herd, including a myriad of outriders none of us could ever keep straight. Jack liked to call us "the little foxes." "Anyway," he went on, "*somebody's* uncle, Wilmarth Lewis, spent his life collecting Horace Walpole, said to me, the other day, about the eighteenth century, his specialty, that, uh, how do you explain how a sort of backwoods country like this, with only three million people, could have produced the three great geniuses of the eighteenth century—Franklin, Jefferson, and Hamilton?"

"Time. They had more of it," I said. "They stayed home on the farm in winter. They read. Wrote letters. Apparently, thought, something no longer done—in public life."

Jack's mind skipped about. "You know in this, uh, job . . . I get to meet everybody—all these great movers and shakers and the thing I'm most struck by the lot of them is how second-rate they are. Then you read all those debates over the Constitution . . . nothing like that now. Nothing." It would be nice if he or I had come to a conclusion that morning but we did not. I did note, like John Adams, that our Constitution and laws were deeply grounded in England: "Anglo-Saxon attitudes," I said.

Jack grunted. Although something of an anglophile, he was still an *Irish* Catholic. "Maybe it was something in the water," he said helpfully. "I wish we had more of it, the water, that is." Then Bobby arrived, on cue. (The Berlin Wall was going up.) I went for a walk on the beach, mildly aware that I was intersecting with history, which has its own tidelike rhythms, unknown to us at the time; and forever after too. Certainly, the inventors of our nation would be astonished at what we have done to their handiwork, their reputations as well.

Ten days before Jefferson died, he wrote some notes for the approaching fiftieth anniversary of his Declaration of Independence. "May it be to the world what I believe it will be . . . the signal of arousing men to burst the chains under which monkish ignorance and superstition had persuaded them to bind themselves, and to assume the blessings and security of self-government. . . . The general spread of the light of science has already laid open to every view the palpable truth that the mass of mankind has not been born with saddles on their backs, nor a favored few booted and spurred, ready to ride them legitimately,

by the grace of God . . . " Science! To us that means total surveillance, electronic devices to track others, weapons of mass . . .

On July 4, 1826, Jefferson died. For posterity he wanted to be
known as the author "of the Declaration of American Independence, the statute of Virginia for religious freedom, and father
of the University of Virginia."

A few hours later, the dying John Adams said, "Thomas Jefferson still lives." But Jefferson had already departed. John Adams
had *his* epitaph ready; it was to the point: "Here lies John Adams,
who took upon himself the responsibility of the peace with
France in the year 1800."

"Let us now praise famous men and our fathers that begat us,"
as the New England hymn of my youth, based on Ecclesiacticus,
most pointedly instructed us. Meanwhile, dear Jack, in the forty
years since your murder, I have pondered your question, and this
volume is my hardly definitive answer.

Index

Acheson, Dean, 47

Adams, Abigail Smith, 36, 70, 101, 107, 108, 131, 159; background of, 35; censoriousness of, 62–63; on Washington, 70; on Britain, 104; on Hamilton, 132–33; on Talleyrand, 150; illness of, 158

Adams, Henry, 175

Adams, John, 27, 45, 91, 113, 146–47; on Hamilton, 17, 133, 169; on Washington, 19; aristocracy mistrusted by, 29–30; on roots of Revolution, 34; marriage of, 35–36; Washington backed by, 38; on southerners, 49–50; on monarchy, 50, 51; on property, 52–53; on French Revolution, 56, 57, 107; Franklin contrasted with, 61; in Europe, 62–63, 67, 97; Franklin on, 64; Jefferson on, 64, 93; election as vice president of, 65, 66, 67–70; election as president of, 66–67, 125; as vice president, 71, 73, 74–75, 129–30; on British constitution, 92; on Genet, 100; on Jefferson, 101–2; threat of war and, 103, 104–5; Jay treaty and, 108–9, 115; Hamilton's rivalry with, 114, 124, 133; inauguration as president of, 134–35, 137; weak start of, 138–39; war with France and, 141, 148–51, 156–57, 158–59; Alien and Sedition Acts approved by, 153–55, 162, 164–65; on the English, 160; French overtures to, 167–68; troubles with cabinet of, 168–71; midnight appointments of, 178–79, 180, 181; death of, 189

Adams, John (the elder), 35
Adams, John Quincy, 60, 73, 102
Adams, Samuel, 130
Adet, Pierre Auguste, 125, 130
Alabama, 56
Alaska, 56, 60
Alexander Hamilton and the Persistence of Myth (Knott), 24
Alexander the Great, 136
Alien and Sedition Acts (1798), 152–55, 156, 160–66
American Indians, 33, 74, 177
American Pageant, The (Kennedy, Cohen, Bailey), 32–33
Anti-Federalists, 4, 23, 49, 53
Argus (newspaper), 117
Arizona, 60
Arnold, Benedict, 40
Articles of Confederation, 3, 5–6, 47
Assumption of state debts, 80, 85–90
Aurora (newspaper), 97

Bache, Benjamin Franklin, 153–54
Bailyn, Bernard, 184–85
Bank of the United States, 90–91, 94
Barber of Seville, The (Beaumarchais), 148
Barras, Paul François Jean Nicolas, vicomte de, 147
Beaumarchais, Pierre Augustin Caron de, 148
Beckmen (Beekman), David, 17
Beckwith, George, 95, 96
Belgium, 149
Benjamin Franklin (Wright), 31

Bill of Rights, 13–14
Blair, Tony, 43–44
Bonaparte, Napoleon, 56, 57–58, 59, 114–15, 141, 147, 148, 149, 159, 163, 180
Boston Tea Party, 34
Bourne, Sylvester, 65
Boylston, Susanna, 35
Breckinridge, John C., 164, 165, 182
Burke, Edmund, 160
Burr, Aaron, 40, 71, 95, 115, 124, 129–30, 132, 141, 143, 160, 171, 176

California, 60
Canada, 33, 36, 39–40, 54, 56
Cavaliers, 48, 49
Celisthenes, 135
Charles I, 49
Charles II, 49
Chase, Salmon P., 163
Cincinnati, Society of the, 8–9, 10, 84, 172
Clinton, George, 21, 23, 25, 72
Columbus, Christopher, 54
Common Sense (Paine), 38
Constitutional Convention, 7–13
Continental Congress, 19, 35–38, 47–48, 65–66
Cosway, Maria, 62
Cosway, Richard, 62–63
Craik, James, 173
Cruger, Nicholas, 17–18
Custis, Martha, 2, 11, 72, 73, 172, 173, 174

Dartmouth College v. Woodward (1819), 184

Declaration of Independence, 4, 13, 31–32, 57
Democracy, 22, 135–36, 186
Du Pont de Nemours, Victor, 155, 158

East India Company, 34
Electoral College, 32, 65–67, 136–37
Ellsworth, Oliver, 134
English civil war, 48–49

Factionalism, 48, 66–67
Fairfax of Cameron, Thomas Fairfax, Baron, 142, 145
Fauchet, Joseph, 118–20, 121
Fawcett, Rachel, 17
Federalist papers, 15–16, 21, 23, 141, 162–63, 185–86
Federalists, 4, 23, 66, 68, 97, 107, 108, 114, 115, 117, 149, 156, 161, 171, 179
First Amendment, 161, 177
First Continental Congress, 35–36
Florida, 55–56, 95, 96
France, French, 33, 34, 38, 139, 149, 150–59
Franklin, Benjamin, 12, 133; Constitution endorsed by, 30–31; pessimism of, 32–33, 48, 80; peace with England negotiated by, 45–46, 63; in Europe, 60–62; Jefferson on, 63–64; on Adams, 154
French Revolution, 56, 99, 130, 180

Gallatin, Albert, 169
Gates, Horatio, 49

Genet, Edmond Charles, 99, 100
George III, 3, 32, 37, 39, 50, 72
Germany, Germans, 33, 37–38
Gerry, Elbridge, 141, 146, 150, 151, 154
Great Britain: parliamentary system in, 29; colonies taxed by, 33–35; France vs., 33, 55; American towns burned by, 38, 39, 41; as maritime power, 45, 56
Greco-Roman culture, 54–55
Grenville, William Wyndham, Lord Grenville, 111–12

Hamilton, Alexander, 143, 146, 147, 172; as Federalist, 5–6, 7, 8, 23–24, 25, 66, 121–22, 149, 179; military career of, 5, 18–20, 106, 115, 140, 143, 151, 152, 156, 157, 158; as author of Federalist papers, 11, 15, 16, 21, 22, 162–63, 185; background of, 17–18; aristocracy defended by, 51; Electoral College viewed by, 65, 136–37; as treasury secretary, 67, 71–72, 79–80, 81; Anglophilia of, 71–72, 81, 92; Jefferson on, 85–86, 88, 90, 91, 94; national bank viewed by, 91; pro-British machinations of, 95, 96–97, 100–101, 105, 111–12, 114, 140; Washington's rebuke of, 98; in Whiskey Rebellion, 106; political maneuvering of, 107, 110, 124, 129–33, 137–38, 169, 170; Napoleon admired by, 115, 151; Jay treaty defended by, 116–17; as author of Farewell Address,

Hamilton, Alexander *(continued)*
121–26; Talleyrand's admiration
for, 141; war with France and,
156, 157, 158, 159, 168
Hamilton, James, 17
Hammond, George, 100–101,
111–12, 118
Hanover, House of, 37
Hardwick, Elizabeth, 175
Harrington, James, 52
Hawaii, 60
Hay, John, 56
Helvétius, Anne, 63
Hemings, Sally, 62, 77, 176
Henry, Patrick, 4, 36, 53, 107, 145
Hessians, 37–38, 39
History of the United States
(H. Adams), 175
Holmes, Oliver Wendell, Jr., 144,
186
Homestead Act (1862), 53
House of Representatives, U.S.,
12, 29
Howe, William, 19
Hume, David, 15

Idaho, 60
Impeachment, 163
Indians, American, 33, 74, 177
Intolerable Acts, 35
Irish, 152
Isolationism, 53–54

Jackson, Andrew, 183
Jacobins, 180
James, William, 186
Jay, John, 5, 21, 23, 45, 63, 68, 114,
117, 129, 178

Jay treaty, 105, 108, 111–19,
139–40, 148
Jefferson, Martha, 76–77
Jefferson, Polly, 109
Jefferson, Thomas, 21, 23, 27, 47,
131, 132, 137, 142, 143, 146, 151,
155, 158, 169, 171; as minister to
France, 4, 6, 56, 62–63, 66, 97;
as author of Declaration of Independence, 13, 28, 32, 57,
188–89; frequent political
change advocated by, 14, 15, 32;
on Hamilton, 17, 85–86, 88, 90,
91, 94, 117; aristocracy mistrusted by, 29, 51; Constitution
endorsed by, 30; at Continental
Congress, 36; election as president of, 40; on French Revolution, 57, 107; Louisiana Purchase
and, 58–60, 78, 175, 183; on
Franklin, 63–64; on Adams,
63–64, 93; Francophilia of, 66;
election as vice president of, 67;
as secretary of state, 68, 76, 77,
86–87, 94–97; Maclay on,
78–79; history rewritten by,
80–83; Washington defended by,
83–84, 91; on assumption of state
debts, 87–90; Washington's rebuke of, 98; on Genet, 100; retirement of, 101, 109–10, 116;
rationalism of, 102–3; Britain
criticized by, 108; political ambi-
tions of, 124–25; inauguration as
vice president of, 134–35; Alien
and Sedition Acts opposed by,
154, 160–66, 182; Confederate
invocation of, 176–77; inaugura-

tion a president of, 179; Marshall vs., 179–80; Adams's midnight appointments and, 181, 183–84; death of, 189
John Adams (P. Smith), 154
Judicial review, 163, 182–84

Kennedy, John F., 187–88
Kentucky, 95
Kentucky Resolutions, 163–64, 165
King, Rufus, 117, 137
Knott, Stephen F., 24
Knox, Henry, 3, 10, 68, 74, 156
Knox, Hugh, 19

Lafayette, Marquis de, 5, 6, 76, 115, 143
La Rochefoucauld, François, duc de, 57
Laurens, Henry, 63
Lavien, John, 17
Lear, Tobias, 173
Lee, Charles, 183
Lee, "Light Horse Harry," 7
Lewis, Wilmarth, 187
Lexington, Battle of, 37
Liberalism, 52
Life of Washington (Marshall), 83, 146, 180–81, 182–83
Lincoln, Abraham, 53, 94, 166, 177–78, 183
Livingston, Robert R., 58, 59, 70
Lloyd, James, 152, 153
Locke, John, 13, 28, 52
Long, Huey, 47
Louis XVI, 5, 56, 140
Louisiana, 58, 59, 95, 96, 167

Louisiana Purchase, 58–60, 78, 175, 183
Lowell, Robert, 175

Maclay, William, 69, 71, 72–73, 74, 78–79
Madison, James, 64, 89, 146, 164; as Federalist, 5, 6, 7, 23, 145; Washington pressured by, 8, 9, 10; temperateness of, 9, 14, 79; on framers' intent, 13–14; as author of Federalist papers, 15, 16, 21, 22, 163, 185, 186; as Republican, 66, 121; tariffs proposed by, 71; loyalty to Jefferson of, 76, 109, 110, 116, 117; assumption of state debts viewed by, 80; threat of war and, 105; Alien and Sedition Acts opposed by, 160–63; as secretary of state, 181
Magna Carta, 45
Malone, Dumas, 176
Marbury, William, 181, 183, 184
Marbury v. Madison (1803), 83, 144, 163, 183–84
Marie Antoinette, 56
Marriage of Figaro, The (Beaumarchais), 148
Marshall, John, 83, 141–47, 149–50, 151, 155–56, 161, 163, 170, 178–85
Mason, George, 13, 27–29, 145
Massachusetts, 6
McCulloch v. Maryland (1819), 185
McHenry, James, 138, 152, 155, 156, 157, 168–69, 171
Mexico, 54, 60, 115
Miscellaneous Notes (Pickering), 120

Mississippi, 56
Missouri Compromise (1857), 184
Monarchism, 48, 50, 51
Monroe, James, 58, 60, 146, 172
Monroe Doctrine, 60
Montaigne, Michel de, 78
Montesquieu, Charles Louis de
    Secondat, Baron de, 186
Montgomery, Richard, 39, 40
Morocco, 78
Morris, Gouverneur, 11, 12, 21,
    144, 182
Morris, Robert, 11
Mount Vernon, 1–2

Nelson, Horatio Nelson, Viscount,
    160
New Hampshire, 24
New Jersey, 61
New Orleans, 58, 59
New York City, 17, 18, 40, 41
New York State, 7, 25, 71
North, Frederick North, Baron, 38
Nullification, 162, 164, 165, 176

Oregon, 60

Paine, Thomas, 38, 39, 45, 130–31
Party system, 97
Pennsylvania, 171
Pericles, 136
Philippines, 60
Pickering, Timothy, 117–19, 120,
    121, 138, 152, 155, 156, 168,
    169–70
Pinckney, Charles, 148, 180; as
    minister to France, 140, 141, 146
Pinckney, Thomas, 129, 137; as vice

presidential candidate, 124, 125;
    mediocrity of, 130, 132
Pitt, William, the Younger, 141
Plague, 54–55
Polk, James K., 60
Portugal, 78
Potomac Company, 2, 4, 113, 117,
    118, 171
Publius Valerius, 22
Puerto Rico, 60
Puritanism, 48, 55

Quebec, 40
Quincy family, 35

Randolph, Edmund, 68, 111,
    117–19, 120, 121
Randolph, Thomas Mann, Jr., 77
Republicanism, 22, 39, 186
Republican Party, 66, 97, 108, 161,
    179
Restoration, 49
Rhode Island, 6
Rights of Man, The (Paine), 130–31
Robespierre, Maximilien, 130
Roosevelt, Franklin, 47
Roundheads, 48–49
Russia, 56, 60

Santo Domingo, 58
Scalia, Antonin, 185
Schuyler, Philip, 20
Schuyler family, 18, 51
Scott, Dred, 184
Second Continental Congress,
    37–38
Senate, U.S., 12, 29–30, 74, 76, 104
Seven Years' War, 34, 38

Shays, Daniel, 6–8, 47
Shays's rebellion, 6–8, 144
Shipley, Jonathan, Bishop, 46
Slavery, 1, 4, 13, 17, 18, 29, 53, 55,
    77, 166, 177
Smith, Abigail. *See* Adams, Abigail
    Smith
Smith, Page, 154
Smith, Melancton, 23, 25
Smith, William Stephens, 155
Society of the Cincinnati. *See*
    Cincinnati, Society of the
Sophocles, 136
Spain, 54, 55, 58, 77, 94–96, 139,
    149
States' rights, 49
Steuart, Sir James, 16
Stevens, John Paul, 185
*Summary View of the Rights of British
    America* (Jefferson), 36
Supreme Court, U.S., 12, 144, 163,
    180

Talleyrand, Charles Maurice de,
    140–41, 146, 147, 148, 149, 156,
    158, 167, 170
Tammany Hall, 40, 71
Taxation without representation,
    22, 33–34, 35
Tennessee, 56
Tenth Amendment, 161
Term limits, 14, 29
Texas, 55
Thatcher, Margaret, 43
Thomas, Clarence, 185
To Begin the World Anew (Bailyn),
    185
Tories, 36, 48

Toussaint L'Ouverture, François
    Dominique, 59
Truman, Harry, 47

Utah, 60

Vermont, 95
Veto power, 12
Virginia: Constitutional Con-
    ventional requested by, 5; state
    constitution of, 13, 27–28;
    Constitution ratified by, 25,
    145–46
Virginia Resolutions, 163
Voting rights, 28–29

Warren, Mercy Otis, 50
Warren Court, 145
Washington, Bushrod, 155
Washington, George, 12, 21, 115,
    133–34, 142, 143, 146, 159,
    169, 176; at Mount Vernon, 1–2,
    149–50; public image of, 2–3,
    9–10, 30; as Federalist, 4, 5, 23;
    on Shays's rebellion, 7–8; at
    Constitutional Convention,
    8–11; Hamilton in employ of,
    18–19, 20; as general, 19, 38,
    40, 142, 143, 151, 155–58;
    marriage of, 36; on Continental
    Congress, 48; election as presi-
    dent of, 67, 129–33; inauguration
    as president of, 68, 70; as presi-
    dent, 72–75, 77, 81; Jefferson's
    defense of, 83–84, 91; "internal
    dissensions" mediated by, 96,
    97–98; neutrality invoked by,
    99–100, 103, 105; Whiskey

Washington, George *(continued)*
Rebellion put down by, 105–6;
Adams and, 108, 130; Farewell
Address of, 110–11, 121–26,
131–32, 170; Jay treaty and,
111–13, 116, 117–20; federal
capital envisioned by, 113–14;
Paine and, 130–31; declining
health of, 158, 171–73; death of,
173–74
Washington, Martha Custis, 2, 11,
72, 73, 172, 173, 174
Washington State, 60
Wayles, John, 77

Wayne, Mad Anthony, 143
Webster, Daniel, 94
Weems, Parson, 9–10
Whiskey Rebellion, 105
Wilkinson, James, 95
Wolcott, Oliver, 118, 120, 121, 138,
159, 168, 169, 170
World War I, 60
Wright, Esmond, 31

XYZ Affair, 147–48

Yellow fever, 149, 158